**DO NOT REMOVE
CARDS FROM POCKET**

The
POWERFUL
PARENT

The
POWERFUL
PARENT

DAVID M. GOTTESMAN, M.D.

APPLETON-CENTURY-CROFTS
Norwalk, Connecticut

82 83 84 85 86 / 10 9 8 7 6 5 4 3 2 1

Prentice-Hall International, Inc., London
Prentice-Hall of Australia, Pty. Ltd., Sydney
Prentice-Hall of India Private Limited, New Delhi
Prentice-Hall of Japan, Inc., Tokyo
Prentice-Hall of Southeast Asia (Pte.) Ltd., Singapore
Whitehall Books Ltd., Wellington, New Zealand

Library of Congress Cataloging in Publication Data

Gottesman, David M., 1940-
  The powerful parent.

  Includes index.
  1. Children—Services for—United States—Evaluation.
2. Parenting—United States. I. Title.
HV741.G65   362.7'95'0973   81-17676

ISBN 0-8385-7863-2   A7863-2
ISBN 0-8385-7862-4 (pbk.)   A7862-4

Text and cover design by Gloria J. Moyer
Photos for chapters 1, 2, and 3 by Timothy H. Raab.
Photo for chapter 4 by Joseph P. Schuyler.

PRINTED IN THE UNITED STATES OF AMERICA

To Susan, who believed in me from the beginning,

*To Julie, Bart, Scott, Jill, and Krissy, who helped me
to learn first hand how to advocate for children,*

To Gertrude and James, who were always there to help,

*To Mark Degnan, M.D., whose untimely death took away
a true advocate for all children.*

Contents

A SPECIAL THANKS TO

Jerry Berger
Arthur Copeland
Kathy Corbat
George Dardani
Stephen Davidson
Frank Doberman
Dale Dorner
Eleanor Roosevelt
    Developmental Services
John Fowler
Robert Freeman

Frank Hardmeyer
John Jehu
Bill Long
Wayne McClintoch
Julie Nelson
Kris Pollard
Len Quint
Ruth Sabo
John Wapner
Jack White
Wildwood School

Introduction

The need to teach parents how to advocate for their children is becoming increasingly necessary. The once simple systems that served a child's physical, social, emotional, legal, and educational needs have become more complicated as well as sophisticated. The previous ways in which a parent could deal directly and understand services no longer exists. Parenting itself has changed greatly over the years. Although the basics remain the same, changing needs of children and earlier understanding of their wants pressure parents to be more sophisticated in their roles and able to advocate for their children so that they can obtain what is both necessary and what is also "best." This handbook is designed to teach parents what to look for when obtaining services for their children, and when dissatisfied, to help them to find constructive alternative options. The basic premise of this handbook rests on the simple fact that in a world of bureaucracy, sophisticated, and, at times, intimidating systems (i.e., school, doctor's offices), a parent, as a consumer has a right to choose what is best for his child, and not just what is offered.

The handbook looks at the physical, social, emotional, legal, and educational needs of children as well as miscellaneous areas and systems that effect your child. It attempts to outline an approach for evaluating those individuals and systems providing service to your child as well as informing you, as a parent, where or how to go about obtaining necessary services. The areas to be covered are as large as the needs of the growing child. The people or agencies involved are those that serve your child directly. You, as parents, will be taught how to evaluate everyone from your child's pediatrician and dentist to your child's teacher. This book is not confined to traditional concepts, but attempts to be flexible enough to shed light on the "new." It will teach you to be the powerful parent.

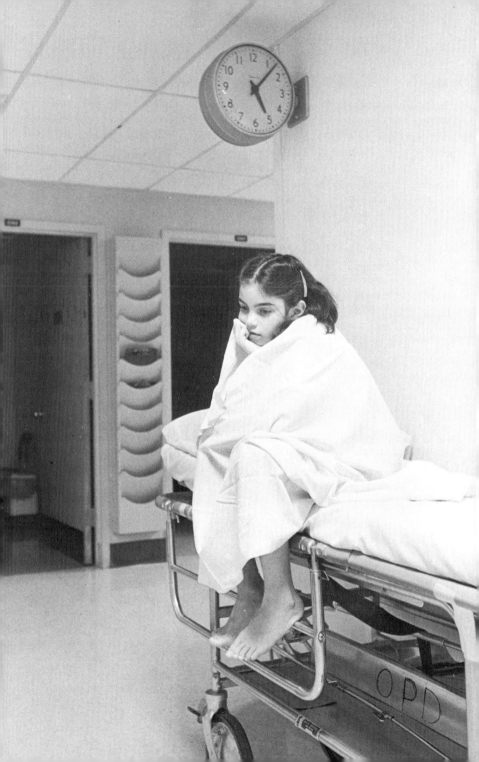

1

Physical Needs of Children

Picking the Right Pediatrician

The pediatrician is your child's doctor. Since he or she will play a major role in the child's life, picking a pediatrician is very important. Pediatricians are chosen three different ways: inheritance, reputation, and recommendation. The inheritance method works this way: "She was my doctor when I was a kid, so I guess I'll use her." The reputation method is based on who your friends, neighbors, or relatives use. Unfortunately, it may be based on reasons ranging from "He's gorgeous" to the fact that he's considered cheap. Some good reasons are, "If I call at night, I get a call back," or "She listens to me." The recommendation method relies on asking your obstetrician whom he or she recommends or asking another professional (not necessarily a physician, but maybe a nurse).

You will need a doctor if you're going to have a baby. (We'll figure out later how to pick a pediatrician in other situations, such as when you're moving or in an emergency.) Pediatricians like new families. Since the birthrate is down, new families assure that the pediatrician will have a patient for eighteen years. Thus, the market value of a patient is high, making it a buyer's market. Regardless of which of the above methods is used, you have to find out certain things before you choose.

1

The first thing you probably want to know is whether the pediatrician is in solo practice or in a group practice. There are advantages and disadvantages to both. The solo pediatrician has the advantage of knowing you better. Basically, you get what you ask for: the doctor. The disadvantages include the fact that the pediatrician may not always be available and give you immediate service in case of an emergency. When the pediatrician is not on call, he or she has coverage from one or several other doctors. Find out who is covering for the doctor and when he or she will be available *ahead of time*. The fewer doctors covering for the pediatrician, the better for your child.

The group pediatrician has good and bad points. Such a doctor can provide better emergency treatment. He or she also is more likely than the solo pediatrician to have a weekend sick call. This is a time-saver for the group pediatrician. The group practice also guarantees that you will know who the guest doctor will be when the on-call system is working. (Remember, the pediatrician has time off.)

There are two kinds of pediatric group practices. The private group is probably well established and run by a staff with a personal commitment. To understand the private group, you must realize that these pediatricians most likely control the financial end of the business. Although they are often salaried, they have a personal economic interest in seeing that the business does well. In dollars and cents, that means the better services the pediatrician provides, the more likely he or she will have a large practice and make more money. The health maintenance organization (HMO) is usually newly established, and the personnel (including your pediatrician) may or may not be available. It may be preferred for the young family, however, because they will be better able to afford quality care. You pay the HMO group on a monthly basis, a fixed rate, whether you use their services or not. Remember, HMOs lock you into the services they offer. Your child has to use *only* the doctors the HMO has on staff (including subspecialists the child may need in the future).

Use the following questions to help you make your choice:

• What are the pediatricians's hours? Office hours should be during the standard workday.

- Will the pediatrician make a weekend sick call? It's nice to have a time during the weekend when you can see the pediatrician. Pediatricians who have weekend hours are often available on Saturday mornings.
- Does the pediatrician have evening hours? This is an important service for working parents.
- Will the pediatrician take a morning call-in? Some pediatricians set aside an hour each morning to speak to patients about their concerns and problems. This practice helps the pediatrician too, because he or she doesn't have to interrupt the workday.
- What is the distance between you and the pediatrician? Don't forget to find out how long it will take you to reach the pediatrician's office. An hour's ride to the office may outweigh the advantage of being able to see a particular doctor or group.
- Make sure you find a pediatrician before your baby is born or your child gets sick. This gives you time to get to know the doctor and, if you are not happy with your choice, to change. It also gives the doctor time to explain what will be happening when he or she sees your child. This is especially important if the child is a newborn or is in the hospital. If there is a problem, you have already met the pediatrician, you already know him, and you can trust him.

Initial Contact

Let's see what happens when you try to get an appointment with a pediatrician for a child who is not a newborn. The initial contact will be made with a receptionist. Nothing turns off a parent more than a discourteous or impatient receptionist. Generally, for a routine appointment, you may have to wait one to three weeks to be seen. If you have to wait much longer than that, the pediatrician is probably overextended. If you call because of a crisis, you should let the receptionist know that you have a real problem and need to talk to a medically trained person. More often than not, it will be the office nurse. If the receptionist hassles you, the thing to say (throughout this book, magic words, or *action words*, will be described) is that you want to speak to the nurse. Say, "My child is quite sick, and I'm very concerned." Often it helps if you ask for someone by name. Know your doctor's nurse by name and ask for her; eventually, you should be able to talk to the pediatrician. Be straightforward and insistent with the nurse. Ask to talk to the pediatrician! The action words here are *good medicine*. Say to the nurse, "I'm sure it is good medicine to have me talk to the doctor."

If you call in the morning with a crisis but can't be seen until the afternoon or can't talk to the pediatrician (and you feel it's a real emergency), use the action words *emergency room*. State matter of factly, "I'll have to take my child to the emergency room and have them call the doctor." This usually speeds things up. Remember, you're paying for the pediatrician's services.

Doctor's Office
The office should be near your home and convenient for you and your child. It should be large enough to accommodate children coming for preventive checkups (routine visits) as well as those who are sick. The waiting room should have toys and play materials for the child. Pediatricians have a habit of falling behind, but you shouldn't have to wait more than fifteen minutes, unless there is an interrupting emergency. The receptionist shouldn't be upset if young children climb on the furniture.

Don't be fooled by expensive waiting rooms. They have to be paid for.

REMEMBER: Service is in the office, not in the waiting room.

A Closer Look at the Pediatrician
The age of the pediatrician is important, especially if he or she is in solo practice. The older physician may not be able to cover a solo practice as well as the younger doctor. Younger pediatricians in a group have the advantage of gaining from the experience of older doctors.

Your child's pediatrician should be certified by the American Academy of Pediatrics, which means that this doctor has fulfilled the minimal training requirements necessary in this field. It is no guarantee, but it's a plus. If you don't see a diploma on the wall or are embarrassed to ask, call the county medical society. They'll be happy to tell you. Ask the pediatrician which hospitals he or she uses. There are two kinds of hospitals the doctor may use if your community is large enough. Teaching hospitals usually are associated with medical schools or at least are certified to have a house staff (doctors in training). Community hospitals usually don't have a teaching affiliation.

What are the advantages and disadvantages of the two types of hospitals? Community hospitals usually have amenities, and the staff members, from doctor to nurse, are often more relaxed and attuned to your needs. The disadvantages are that certain technologies won't be available because of cost (e.g., people to run certain diagnostic machines as well as the machines themselves).

Teaching hospitals can have staff members ranging from student nurses to student doctors (possibly medical students) and doctors in training (beyond medical school). That means that you and your child will have to put up with answering the same questions many times. Medical sophistication, however, is better than average, and the house staff often can write orders that get things done faster. Overall, it's the place to be for complicated cases, and you should discuss this with the pediatrician should you need to hospitalize the child.

Checklist for rating a pediatrician:

☐ Respects the parent
☐ Respects the child
☐ Listens to the parent and the child patiently
☐ Puts the child and parent at ease

☐ Explains things to the child and you so that you understand them

Checklist for rating yourself as a parent:

☐ You ask questions if you don't understand.
☐ You feel silly after the pediatrician leaves; you say to yourself, "I wish I had asked."
☐ You have the doctor explain to your child in the child's language what's wrong.

☐ You get the pediatrician to listen to your parent's intuition. The action word here is *my own child*. You should ask, "Don't you think I know my own child?"
☐ You are impressed by the pediatrician's personality and competence. (The doctor's ability to handle your child in a reasonable and systematic fashion and to explain to *you* what's wrong.)

The pediatrician should find out about your pregnancy and your child's delivery (if this is the first visit), feeding history, previous illnesses, and early growth and development (when the child walked, talked, smiled, etc.). If the doctor doesn't bring it up, you should, especially at the first visit. The pediatrician should ask questions about the various parts of the body and about any problems with the stomach or movement of the arms and legs. He or she should ask about illnesses that run in the family. If questions get too personal, ask why the doctor wants to know before you answer. Remember, the pediatrician needs to know as much as possible to help your child.

How much time should the pediatrician give you? An evaluation of a well child or one with a minor illness should take, on the average, fifteen minutes. More complicated problems may require more time. Be prepared to pay. If you want more time, prior to a visit ask the pediatrician how much that visit will cost. Tell the doctor why you want the time. Counseling time (problems of a behavioral, emotional, or social nature) may be set aside, and the pediatrician may also have a special time of the week for doing that work.

If you are afraid to ask a question of the pediatrician, you have to look at the possibility that there is something wrong between you. Ask what you don't know. You're entitled to an answer. If the doctor is evasive, press on. There is nothing wrong if the doctor says that he or she doesn't know. The doctor may not know all the answers. An action word to use is *second opinion*. Say, "Maybe you need time to get a second opinion." The doctor should respond by saying, "I'll get you the answer, and call you later." Call if he or she doesn't call you. Watch out for the know-it-all, who may know nothing.

Let's say you are not happy with the pediatrician and want to change. First, weigh the pluses and the minuses of the relationship. The grass is *not* always greener elsewhere. Talk to the pediatrician. Explain what you don't like. Be specific. Perhaps you are unhappy with the on-call system, the office staff, or the pediatrician's handling of you or your child. Get the doctor's reaction. If you're still not happy, look elsewhere. Should you find a new doctor, call the first doctor's receptionist and ask that a copy of your records be forwarded to the new pediatrician. Put this request in writing. If the old pediatrician calls, explain the situation again. Remember to find out more this time. You may be jumping from the frying pan into the fire.

Special Situations

If you are out of town and require emergency medical care for your child, you probably will have to use the local hospital. Ask for a pediatrician. Later on in this book, we will discuss how to deal with the emergency rooms and its staff.

The answering service can be the most aggravating part of your contact with a pediatrician and may lead you to choose another pediatrician. What is a reasonable time to wait for a call back? The answering service should give you an accurate assessment of the time before the pediatrician will call back. Ask the answering service to be specific. They may be able to tell you that you will have a long wait because of an emergency. If your problem is urgent, tell the answering service. If you have a bad experience with the service, tell the pediatrician so that he or she can correct the situation. It's part of the doctor's public relations. If you don't hear within the time stated by the answering service, call back. Keep calling back until you get a reply. You may have to use the action words *emergency room* again. Say to the answering service (especially if you feel that the child is getting sicker), "I will have to take my child to the emergency room and tell the doctor that you couldn't reach him."

At times the pediatrician may want to perform what seems to be yet another test on the child. Ask whether the test results will change the diagnosis or treatment plan. The action words to stop the test is *guinea pig*. State, "I don't want my child to be used as a *guinea pig*." The pediatrician should think twice before subjecting your child to unnecessary tests.

When you are moving, ask the people in the area where you're going who they use. You will have to rely on reputation. Take copies of the child's records with you to be sure that they get there. Contact the new pediatrician's office when you get to the new area. This is check-out time, and you will have to repeat this all over again (sick call, the hospitals the doctor uses, etc.).

It never hurts to ask for free samples. Drug companies provide them to pediatricians. But don't expect the doctor to have enough for the whole illness or in convenient forms. Remember, the doctor may give you what is available rather than the best drug. Don't be afraid to ask. Always ask about diet restrictions as they relate to the drugs your child is taking. Some foods interfere with certain drugs. Always ask the pediatrician when he or she writes a prescription whether you can get the drug in its generic form instead of by trade name. You pay more for the trade-name drug, and it may not be better than the generic. Always ask about the *side effects* of the drugs your child is taking.

Always ask for a list of charges. At the first visit, ask about the billing system. You may have to pay at each visit, and so you will want to ask about payment when you call the office the first time. Find out before you go in order to prevent embarrassment. You may be able to work out your own system for payments, which you must honor.

The American Academy of Pediatrics has a great deal of parent education information, usually free of charge. It includes such information as how to select a car seat, formula feeding, and vitamins. Write to:

American Academy of Pediatrics
1801 Hinman Avenue
Evanston, Ill. 60204

Every state has a medical society, and usually each smaller district (county) has a local medical society. They can be helpful in finding speakers for PTAs or telling you more about the pediatrician. Also, they are there for complaints.

POINTS TO REMEMBER

• Pick a pediatrician before you need his or her services.
• You can pick a pediatrician three different ways: inheritance, reputation, or recommendation. Recommendation is the best method, followed by reputation.
• In evaluating a pediatrician, take a close look at the office, the receptionist, the office nurse, and the doctor's personal qualities.
• You can change your pediatrician.

• Action words to remember: *emergency room, second opinion, good medical practice (good medicine), guinea pig, my own child, your doctor's name.*

Review of Situations in Which You Use the Action Words

1. To get past the answering service, say, "I'll let the doctor know I waited this long," or "I'll take my child to the emergency room, since I can't wait any longer. I'll let the doctor know you couldn't reach him."
2. To get past the receptionist, say, "My child is quite sick." If need be, say, "I'll have to take my child to the emergency room and call the doctor."
3. To get past the office nurse, say, "I'm sure the doctor would want to talk to me personally, since that's good medicine."
4. If your questions are not being answered directly, say, "If you'd like to get a second opinion, we'd be happy to pay for it."
5. If the pediatrician isn't listening to you or taking your "intuition" into account, say, "Don't you think I know my own child?"
6. When the pediatrician suggests additional tests, ask, "Are these tests going to change your diagnosis or treatment?" If the doctor says, "No, we're doing it for completeness," say, "I feel like my child is being used as a guinea pig."

Emergency Room

At some time your child will need to use a hospital emergency room. As the name implies, the emergency room is intended for use in an emergency medical need. Yet today, many parents use the emergency room as an outpatient pediatric clinic; if they are unable to see the pediatrician during the week, on weekends, or at night, they take the child to the emergency room for medical treatment. Probably only twenty percent of all people seen in a busy emergency room require emergency medical care. In an actual emergency (your child breaks a bone or is cut badly enough to require stitches), the decision to use the emergency room is clear. It is less clear when the child develops a high fever that does not respond to usual medical treatment and you cannot reach the pediatrician. There are times when you will need the services of the emergency room because pediatric medical care is not available. This is certainly true if you are on vacation, away from the child's usual pediatrician.

The time to use the emergency room is dictated by two situations. The first is when a true emergency exists and immediate medical intervention is necessary. The second is when a medical situation arises, which, if not attended to, could lead to a medical emergency, and your usual medical resources are not available. The decision to use the medical resources of the emergency room must be weighed against the following considerations:

• The resources of the emergency room vary from hospital to hospital. Different emergency rooms have different staffing patterns: some are staffed by physicians, other by nurses and physician assistants with doctors on call. Thus, some emergency rooms may have no doctors immediately available so that the first person seeing your child is a nurse. A doctor can then be called if necessary. Some emergency rooms employ an emergency-room physician who has been specially trained in medical emergencies, yet this doctor may not be experienced in pediatric emergencies. Should you use an emergency room that is part of a teaching hospital, the physician you see may be in training at that hospital as an intern or resident. You should not expect to be seen by a fully trained doctor, let alone a pediatric specialist, in an emergency room.

• The sophistication of the diagnostic equipment can vary greatly. For instance, certain blood work that may be routinely available in one hospital emergency room may not be available *at all* in another.

• Although you may consider the medical problem an emergency, the emergency-room staff may not view it the same way. For instance, your child may be running a high fever, but compared to a fractured skull it may not be as much of an emergency. This may be reflected in how fast the child is seen and how long you have to wait.

When you decide that the child needs the emergency room, it is important to first call ahead if possible. If you have been in touch with the child's pediatrician and he or she suggests using the emergency room, ask the pediatrician to call ahead and notify the emergency-room staff that you are coming in and for what reason. This is helpful to the child because it notifies the staff that your pediatrician has a personal interest in this case. Furthermore, it allows the pediatrician to share information with the emergency-room staff and to give instructions as to what tests or procedures should be carried out. If the child needs follow-up care or the pediatrician wants a specific physician to see the child, the pediatrician can leave instructions when calling ahead. This helps to ensure that your child will be cared for by physicians whom the pediatrician respects. If the pediatrician is not available and you have to advocate alone for your child in the emergency room, make the call yourself. You will want the following to occur:

• You will state to the emergency-room staff the nature of the child's emergency. Often, the staff will make suggestions about alternative care for the child.

• You will want to find out how busy the emergency room is when you call, realizing that the number of people using the emergency room can change from moment to moment. If you are informed that the emergency room is very busy, you may want to use the services of another one or delay going. Obviously, if it is a life or death emergency, your child may become a priority patient and be the first in line.

• The emergency-room staff may be able to notify your pediatrician if you haven't, thus informing him or her that you are bringing the child to the emergency room. If you are using an emergency room and the pediatrician cannot be involved, calling ahead allows the staff the opportunity to notify specialists or obtain and prepare any special equipment the child may need. For instance, if you believe that the child has croup (a respiratory illness associated with difficulty breathing), calling ahead allows the emergency room staff to prepare the pediatric floor for the possible use of a croup tent. This is better than having the child wait while they make preparations. Also, the emergency room may refer you to a different one where specialists or special equipment is available. (Remember, not all facilities have all the people and equipment your child may need, and saving time might save your child's life.)

On the way to the hospital, talk to the child about what to expect. (Obviously, in some emergencies that is not possible.) Explain what the medical problem is, why you and the child are going to the emergency room, the possible people who will take care of the child, and, to the best of your knowledge, the type of examination the child may be given. If you believe that the child will need tests, talk about x-rays and blood tests. How you inform the child may make the difference between a cooperative child and a hysterical one. How much you say will also depend on the child's age; you may say less to a younger child than to an older one. Once you arrive at the emergency room, you will need to do the following:

• Identify your child to the emergency room. If you have called ahead yourself or if the pediatrician has called ahead, let the emergency-room staff know. Use the pediatrician's name often. You need to have medical information about the child available, such as any previous care for the same illness, date of immunizations or operations, allergies, and significant other history.

• Notify the emergency-room staff that you would like the child to be seen by a pediatrician, not an "adult" doctor. A staff doctor may treat the child for something like a broken arm. However, a pediatrician should be involved. A pediatrician has general medical information about the care of children that a general physician in the emergency room may not have, such as the usual medications and dosages appropriate for children. Again, you have to remember that the emergency room you choose may not have a pediatrician on call in the hospital. You may initially choose to use the medical staff offered by the emergency room and make a decision later on as to whether you will rely just on these individuals. In a teaching hospital, you may also start out by using an intern or resident (doctors in training) and later involve a pediatrician.

REMEMBER: You want the highest level or competency and training in the medical staff treating your child. A general physician may see the child initially, and then you may ask to have the child seen by a pediatrician. On the other hand, if the child breaks an arm, a pediatrician may be initially involved, but then you will want the child seen by an orthopedic surgeon. You may ask initially: "Is this problem something that a pediatrician needs to care for?" The question puts the emergency-room staff on notice that you know that pediatricians are more familiar with childhood illnesses.

• One of the papers you will have to sign so that your child will receive medical care in the emergency room is the permission sheet. Before signing it, *under any circumstances* (whether a usual medical emergency or a life and death situation), read it carefully. Print under your signature the following: "I want all procedures to be done on my child discussed with me before they are performed." This helps to ensure that you will be involved in all decision-making processes concerning the child's medical care. Should a life or death situation arise that requires life-saving procedures, the emergency room is still protected from any legal action by you should the staff not have time to discuss the situation with you.

• If you are asked to wait or placed in a booth before being seen, you should ask: "How long a wait do you think my child will have?" An appropriate answer by the medical staff would be some specific time period: "You will have to wait twenty minutes." At this point, you have to let the emergency-room staff know that you are worried about the child. You do this by stating: "I'm concerned about his high temperature," or "Do you think that is too long to wait, given her high temperature?" The question is meant to get the busy emergency-room staff members to rethink the situation and to ensure that they have given it adequate thought. The emergency-room staff person may then say to you, "If anything changes while you're waiting, let me know." This paves the way for you to communicate any changes in the child's condition should it change. If you have to wait longer than you expected, you can recontact that emergency-room staff person.

REMEMBER: Even if the emergency-room staff doesn't make that statement, you can.

• The medical person who first examines you child (whether it is the doctor or a nurse) should do so privately, given that the emergency room is not packed, with all available space taken, and that your child's problem is not a life and death matter. If the medical person attempts to examine the child in public (in the waiting room), state: "I would rather that my child be examined in privacy."

REMEMBER: Adults are not examined in full view of other people. Why should your child? Furthermore, your child, no matter how well prepared, will be scared. Privacy helps both the child and you. If the staff person persists, state the following: "My child will be more cooperative if all these people aren't around." Don't give in unless there is no other way.

• Whoever examines your child should introduce himself to your child as well as to you. If the person introduces himself to you as Dr. R. and you don't know who he is, ask: "Are you a pediatrician?" If the person says no, say, "I was hoping my child would be seen by a pediatrician." The doctor should be able to explain to you why he rather than a pediatrician is examining your child (he may be the only physician in the emergency room). Should the person not be a doctor but a physician's assistant, find out when the pediatrician will see your child. The same holds true for a teaching hospital if the child is being seen first by a doctor in training.

REMEMBER: Your child will be seen in the emergency room by whomever is available. You may have to accept what is offered rather than what might be expected under nonemergency circumstances. If the person fails to introduce himself or herself but proceeds to examine your child, say to the child, "I'm sure that the doctor meant to introduce himself to you." The person examining the child should get the hint.

REMEMBER: The way you relate to your child may set the tone for how the emergency-room staff and the person examining the child relate to him or her. The examiner should explain while examining your child what he or she is doing. Essentially, that person should act as you would want the child's pediatrician to act. If the person examining your child doesn't explain, you can state, "It would be helpful to (the child's name) if you would explain what you're doing. She won't be as nervous." Stay with the child for a general examination. Your absence could be upsetting. Even if the emergency room staff members ask you to leave, insist that you stay. If there is an overriding reason, let them explain it to you. But except for some diagnostic procedures, there is little reason why you can't be present. Also, it is very important that your child be treated with dignity. Many times, your child may be treated inappropriately simply because emergency-room staff members do not believe that what they do or how they act toward the child is important. If you feel that the child is being treated in a manner that you yourself would not like, let the emergency room staff and the person examining your child know. Say the following, "I'm concerned that (your child's name) not be embarrassed."

REMEMBER: Stay calm, if not for your own sake, for your child's.

One technique to use to remind the medical staff members how you feel they should relate to your child is through reminders. The following will give you some ideas:

- "I hope that you will keep (your child's name) covered while you examine her."
- "Will you be shielding (name) if he gets x-rays?"
- "I'm sure that before you do any tests you can explain them to us both."
- "(Your child's name) will be less frightened if you explain things to him."

The doctor should pick up on these points. If not, you may have to be even more direct.

REMEMBER: It may be better for you to set the example of how you want others to treat your child than to react angrily.

Finding an Ally
Emergency rooms can be frightening and confusing places. At such times, it is very important to identify as soon as possible a medical ally, a person who works in the emergency room and is familiar with and knowledgeable about its workings. That person should also know the medical staff who will care for the child. The most obvious person is the charge nurse in the emergency room. He or she will have direct contact with those who will care for your child, will be familiar with the personalities and skills of the doctors, and will be able to appraise the medical situation on the basis of experience.

Although the doctor caring for your child must and will talk to you directly, he or she may not be able to do so as often as you might like. Thus, the ally can translate and transmit information to you. This is especially true if the child is seriously injured or critically ill. The ally may at times be the only person who can gather information and keep you informed.

You might start out once you arrive at the emergency room by asking the nurse involved, "Could you help me understand what is going on?" The response of the nurse will tell you how willing he or she is to play this role. At times, someone in a lesser capacity will be more willing but less able to discuss with any authority the medical status of your child. The nurse may inadvertently suggest another medical staff member with whom you can ally yourself. Obviously, the more serious the medical condition your child has, the greater the need to find an ally as soon as possible. This is especially true if you are out of town and find yourself in an unfamiliar emergency room where you are not knowledgeable about the medical personnel who will care for your child.

REMEMBER: The ally is less threatened by the doctors and the emergency-room situation, and so the ally can ask the important questions. The answers the ally gets may also be more to the point because the medical staff feels less threatened than if you, the parent, asked the same questions.

In review, you have done the following up to this point:

1. You have called ahead or have had the child's pediatrician call ahead to the emergency room.
2. Arriving at the emergency room, you have asked that the child be seen by a pediatrician or a specialist specifically trained to deal with the child's medical emergency.

   Because of time (the emergency is of such a critical nature that there may not be enough time to find the specialist) or because the specialist is not available, you may have to allow the available staff to treat your child. However, when the situation is less critical, the advice and direct involvement of the specialist should be considered.
3. You have set the ground rules under which you would prefer that your child be treated:

• The child should have a private examination, not in the waiting room or hallway.

• Your child (if old enough to understand) should be told about each step of the examination.

• All tests and diagnostic procedures should be discussed with you and, when appropriate, with the child.

4. You have identified an ally among the emergency-room staff, preferably the charge nurse, who will be available on a more frequent basis than the physician to help you understand what is occurring and to help gather information about your child.

Treatment Plan

Emergency rooms are used for treatment of medical emergencies. In some situations, there just will not be enough time to fully discuss all of the treatments necessary to help your child. Some of them may have to be done in order to keep the child alive. More likely, you will use the emergency room for medical treatment of a non-critical illness or injury. Thus, there should be adequate time for you to be involved in the discussion of a treatment plan for your child. In discussing treatment, you will want to keep in mind the following:

• Have the doctor go over all the findings, including the results of examinations and any laboratory tests (blood tests or x-rays) that led to his or her conclusions. This should lead up to the doctor telling you what's wrong with your child (the diagnosis) or the extent of any injury. Ask specifically, "Is there anything else that I need to know?" If you are not satisfied with the answer, ask, "I'm not sure I understand everything you have told me. Would you please go over it again?"

REMEMBER: Make sure the results of any tests and the doctor's conclusions are put into simple language, not medical jargon. Do not be afraid to ask "dumb" questions. You may not be thinking as clearly as you would like.

• The results of the tests and examination should lead to a diagnosis or clarify the extent of the injury. Once this is determined, a treatment plan can be formulated. Before the treatment plan is discussed, ask the following: "Have you discussed my child's condition with any other physician or specialist?" By asking this question, you let the medical staff know that you are aware that emergency-room staff members usually have available additional resources that they can call upon in emergency situations. If the reply is no, say, "I would like to have a second opinion." In making this statement, you are giving permission to the medical staff to call in a specialist (if one has not yet been involved) as well as notifying the staff that you want the best possible treatment for your child. If there are no specialists available, you have to accept the available treatment. If specialists are available, you have to wait for them to arrive. When time is not a factor, it is worth the wait. For instance, the repair of most facial lacerations by a plastic surgeon is preferable to treatment by any other medical staff, despite the wait and the possible expense. Furthermore, having your child seen by a specialist should give you greater peace of mind. When you ask the emergency-room staff members about the possibility of getting a second opinion, they may only need to call the consultant on the phone. You can ask, "Would it be possible for me to talk to the consultant so that I can better understand what is wrong with my child?"

When you do speak to the specialist, first say, "Thank you for talking with me." Then ask the following: "Is this a serious problem?" "Do you need to come in to see my child?" "Is this the usual treatment for this problem?" "I hope you will bill me for your time."

REMEMBER: When you talk with the specialist, your child has received additional care that must be paid for.

• Regardless of the treatment, always ask: "Is this the usual treatment for this condition?" By asking this question, you may find out more information about the problem. If the reply is that the treatment is unusual, it may tell you that the child's problem is more severe or the extent of injury greater than you had been led to believe.

Your child may be in great pain. It is important that you remind the doctor prescribing the treatment plan to consider pain medication. Your child may not be able to explain to the doctor the nature and extent of his or her discomfort.

REMEMBER: At any time, you can ask your ally: "I'm not sure I understand everything I've been told. Could you explain it to me?" Treatment should always include the following:

1. *Follow-up.* Your child should be seen within twenty-four hours, if necessary by a specialist if he or she has not been treated by one in the emergency room. If you don't have a specialist (pediatrician or orthopedic surgeon), ask for a referral. Ask, "Who would you use if it were your child?" Many emergency rooms have on-call lists, which are lists of specialists who cover the emergency room during specific periods of time (usually on a monthly basis). It allows the hospital to make referrals without considering the individual ability of the doctor next on the list. (All doctors on the list should be licensed and approved by the hospital.) After you are given a name, ask: "Is this doctor good with children?" "Does he have a lot of experience in these types of situations?" "Is this the doctor you would use?" Your ally may have additional information about the doctor. Wait and find out.
2. *Complications or normal course of the illness.* You will want to find out any problems that could arise from the illness or injury and know what to look out for. You should always ask what you should do if something happens unexpectedly. You should know how to care for the illness or injury over its normal course.
3. *Drugs.* Any drugs prescribed should be discussed in the following context: "Please tell me why that drug was chosen?" "Is the drug absolutely necessary?" "What are the side effects of the drug that I should be aware of?" "Is this a costly drug? Can you prescribe it generically?"
4. *Written instructions.* Most emergency rooms have written instructions concerning complications, drugs, etc. If they don't, say, "You have told me a great deal. Could you please write it down?"

Additional Points to Consider

Foreign Physicians. Many emergency rooms employ foreign physicians. These doctotrs have passed the state medical examination. The question is not their competency but their ability to help you to understand the nature of your child's illness or injury. You may need to have someone, such as the ally, help you fully understand what the doctor is saying. Remember, this may not always be the case.

Admission to the Hospital. Should the child need to be admitted to the hospital after being seen in the emergency room, you must consider the following points:

1. If this is an emergency room away from your hometown, you may want to contact the child's pediatrician or family doctor. He or she should be able to advise you and possibly help you find the best doctor available to treat the child.
2. If you have a pediatrician, you may prefer that your child be admitted under his or her care. Simply say, "I would like my child to be admitted to Dr. R. and have her notified."

You may want this done even if the child needs care that his or her pediatrician doesn't provide, such as surgery. If the child needs to be admitted to a new doctor, you will have to make the decision about which doctor by asking the questions you used when you were looking for a specialist.

Review
1. Make sure you have as much information as possible before making a decision. Don't make a decision if you do not feel you fully understand what is happening.
2. If you are not comfortable making a decision at any point, say: "Is this a decision I have to make right now or do I have some time to think it over?"
3. How you act toward your child will help set the tone for others in their relationships with the child. Stay calm, if not for your own sake, for the child's.
4. Never be afraid to ask a question or to question a decision that the emergency-room staff has made.
5. If in the end you are not happy with the treatment the child is receiving, you have the option of going to another emergency room. That will have to be weighed against the consequences, such as the inconvenience of moving a sick child, the danger of moving an injured child, and the overall emotional stress on the child.

Hospital Stay

At some time during childhood, your child will probably require hospitalization. The child may have to be hospitalized because of an emergency (injury or illness) or because of a need for services that only a hospital can provide (special tests or planned surgery). One-half of all hospitalized children are there for surgical procedures. In either case, hospitalization can be very traumatic for a child. The unpleasant memory of staying in the hospital can last a lifetime. Although it is important to recognize that it would be almost impossible to remove all the anxiety a child will feel as a result of staying in the hospital, your child's stay can be made more successful. Its degree of success will depend a great deal on you. Obviously, some of the steps you can take to ensure that your child's stay in the hospital will be as good as possible will not be available if the child is hospitalized on an emergency basis. However, even under those circumstances, knowing the right questions to ask may bring better success for the child both medically and emotionally.

When the decision is made that your child needs hospitalization, you and the pediatrician should sit down and discuss where the child will be hospitalized. If your community has only one hospital and the child does not require special facilities or care, your choice may be simplified. It is important to remember that if the child needs special facilities or care, you may have to find a hospital that is outside the community and probably less convenient for you.

Picking the Hospital

In choosing a hospital, it is very important to consider both the needs of the child and the procedures the child will require in the hospital. The child's age at the time of hospitalization is another important factor to consider. The newborn or infant may not require the presence of a parent as much as the preschooler. The adolescent's needs are different from those of the younger child. If the child is in the age range of one and a half years to ten years, he or she may demand greater involvement of you. For the young child, these are the years when separation anxiety is greatest and the ability to deal objectively with facts and situations has not yet developed. By nine years of age, the child has enough maturity to perceive the situation but has not yet adequately developed either the emotional or cognitive ability to fully understand what is happening. In many situations, once the child is old enough to recognize what is happening, you become an interpreter of the events that will be occurring.

What to Know in Picking the Hospital

Children's hospital versus a general hospital. Your child does not have to be hospitalized in a children's hospital to receive good medical care. Most communities do not have a hospital specializing only in children's needs. Children's hospitals are usually found only in large metropolitan cities and attract difficult or unusual medical cases. Furthermore, some highly specialized surgical procedures may require expensive equipment, thus precluding their availability in a general community hospital. If the pediatrician leads you to believe that your child may require special tests or care, ask, "Would it be to my child's advantage to be in a children's hospital?"

REMEMBER: Your child can be hospitalized initially in a children's hospital. Later, if the recuperation period is long, the child can be transferred to a local hospital.

Living In. Although opinions about staying with your child in the hospital around the clock vary, it is very important that you do so. If the child is to be hospitalized for a long period of time, you may not have to stay and sleep in the hospital the entire time. As the child becomes accustomed to the hospital, and the procedures (medical and surgical) are completed, your presence may not be required as much as in the initial hospitalization period. However, it is very important to find out ahead of time the hospital staff's feelings about living in. Does the hospital encourage it, or even allow it? In the former case, the hospital appears to want living in, while in the later situation, the hospital tolerates it. In either case, work something out. Should your child require the use of the intensive care unit, find out ahead of time whether they encourage visiting. It is very comforting and reassuring for your child to have you present. Many an anxious child has been calmed by the presence of a parent rather than by drugs.

Visiting Hours. Although the child's friends and relatives should abide by visiting hours, you should have free access, especially if the child is in a hospital that does not allow living in. As a parent, you understand your child's illness as well as his or her temperament. For you, the time with your child in the hospital is a learning experience. It helps you to treat your child better once he or she returns home. Observing the medical care the child receives from the hospital staff will help you understand more clearly what to look for and what to do for the child when he or she leaves the hospital. By talking with the hospital staff about the treatment, you will decrease your anxiety and thus be more comfortable in helping the child.

Teaching Hospital versus Community Hospital. Your community may have both a teaching hospital and a general community hospital. The teaching hospital usually has a house staff of licensed doctors still in training. A teaching hospital may also be associated with a medical school where students are in the process of becoming licensed doctors. Teaching hospitals have the advantage of usually having specialists who deal almost exclusively with children. This can be in areas ranging from pediatric radiology to pediatric anesthesiology. Teaching hospitals have house staff available twenty-four hours a day. This means that if your child should need a doctor during the night, one is available. In the community hospital, the physician cannot be present twenty-four hours. The presence of house staff provides a check and balance system for the treatment of your child. Although your child's doctor makes the final decisions, the house staff's questions should force him or her to consider all possible treatment options, including the most up-to-date possibilities.

REMEMBER: If your child is referred for hospitalization, always have the pediatrician or whoever is making the referral do so to a specific doctor rather than to the hospital in general. Sometimes the doctor may suggest hospitalization for your child by sending you to the emergency room. It is best that your child be referred to a specific doctor.

To help the child get through a stay in the hospital, it is very important that you have an overview of what is to happen each day the child is in the hospital. Since you will hear many new names and diagnostic tests, have a pad and pencil on hand to keep notes. As things are being explained to you, you can write them down and review them later. Furthermore, writing things down as they are being explained forces the medical staff to take the time to discuss them with you and shows that you have more than just a casual interest in what will be happening to the child.

Since children are used to daily structure and thrive within it, it is necessary for you to help establish a daily routine while your child is in the hospital. By knowing the structure ahead of time, you can help ensure that mistakes are not made. You will know how to best prepare the child for any medical tests or procedures he or she may need. In order to outline each day's events ahead of time, it is important to establish with your child's doctor a routine for communicating. This should be established in the doctor's office for a preplanned hospital admission, or on admission in the case of an emergency. In either case, you should say to the doctor: "Won't you sit down and talk with me."

Let the doctor know that you will want to talk on a daily basis. Once in the hospital, set up a consistent time to talk with the doctor. This can be at the same time the doctor or associates make rounds (usually in the morning or late in the afternoon). In this way, the doctor expects to see you, and you expect to see the doctor.

Structuring Your Child's Hospital Day

Your child's hospital day should include the following:

If any specialists are being asked to consult with your child, you should know who they are and why they are being asked to see the child. Ask the doctor: "What will Dr. R. be able to tell us that we don't already know?" If another specialist shows up rather than the doctor you were told would be seeing your child, you have the right to ask: "What happened to Dr. R.? I was expecting her." Let your usual doctor know who came to examine your child. The doctor too may have been expecting someone else.

REMEMBER: You're paying for the consultation.

If another doctor shows up to examine your child, state your confusion: "Dr. R. did not tell me that you would be examining my child. I would like to check with her first." If the doctor gives you a reasonable explanation, you may allow him to examine your child for the sake of time. If you are not satisfied, contact your child's doctor. Let her know that you do not expect to be surprised.

Each day, find out what tests or procedures will be done to the child. Ask, "Does my child need any special preparation for these tests?" Special preparation may include not eating before a blood test or saving urine. Many a blood sample has been taken from a screaming child, only to have the doctor find out that certain precautions were not taken and the blood test would have to be repeated. If medical staff members come to perform a test that has not been scheduled, ask them, "Are you sure that Dr. P. has ordered this test? Dr. R. and I go over each day's events, and this was not one of them." (Show your notebook). If you need to, check with the child's doctor or with the head nurse on the floor.

Whenever possible, follow your child. Some tests, such as x-rays, are done elsewhere in the hospital. By going with the child, you can remain supportive. This may require insistence on your part. There are different opinions as to whether parents should be present when children are undergoing tests. There is really no reason you can't be present, although some tests, because they appear much worse than they are, may be better performed without your presence. Ask the doctor ahead of time. On some occasions, it is better that you not participate. This allows you to provide tender loving care once the tests have been performed.

When will tests, examinations, and procedures be done to your child? It is important to have an idea of when things will be happening so that you can determine the order. If things are done out of order, it is important that you ask: "Dr. R. told me to expect the following. . . . Is it possible that someone has made a mistake?" Knowing when your child is going to be tested or have a procedure done allows you to prepare the child. It is important that the child *not be surprised*. Although the very young child is not fully prepared to understand what may happen, it is very important that you try to explain as much as the child can understand. When you surprise your child, you break the child's trust in you. This breaking of trust or taking by surprise often leads to very bad memories of hospitalization in later life. Should the child have to be hospitalized again, how you handle this first hospitalization may determine how subsequent hospitalizations turn out.

Your ability as a parent to have a good understanding of the child's daily structure while in the hospital cannot be overemphasized. At times, you may be the common thread or link in what can become a chaotic environment. Hospitals, given the variety of children they have to care for, can be hectic and stressful places. The people who staff them, while professional, are only human. Mistakes are made; oversights are not unusual. Understaffed hospitals have to set priorities of care; often they may have to neglect those who are not critically ill. Hospital care is based on shifts of employment. While hospitals have a set of mechanisms for transfer of information from one shift of employees to another, it is subject to breakdown. Thus, it is important to help the child adapt to the hospital cycle. Many parents wonder why they seem to get the rush treatment, only to realize after a great deal of aggravation that they have asked for information and demanded interventions during the "rush" part of the cycle pattern (such as asking for information at the same time the hospital staff is changing shifts). Like every other business, hospitals provide staff based on expected need: more in the daytime, less at night.

Understanding your child's schedule of events allows you to both speed up and slow down the occurrence of events as necessary. Many times, you may provide the checks and balances, the reconsideration of a decision if it does not fit into the schedule you and the doctor have previously planned.

Finding an Ally

It is important that you find an ally among the hospital staff. This person should be of the highest level of competence. In most situations, it may be the head nurse on the pediatric floor where the child is staying. Because you may have questions that must be answered when the child's doctor is not present (your child is just *one* of the doctors patients), this ally can provide an alternative. The higher the level of competency, the greater the authority you can attribute to the information received. When the child's schedule of events does not coincide with the plan you and the doctor have determined, the ally should be able to supply the missing answers. The ally can provide not only formal information but informal opinions that may give you additional insight into the child's illness, the workings of the hospital, and things you can do and cannot do without permission, as well as being supportive to you.

What to Do When You're Not Happy

There will be times, when you will not be happy with the care, the events, or your understanding of what is wrong with your child. If you're not happy, speak with the doctor. Insist that the doctor sit down with you. Despite the doctor's busy schedule, he or she is aware that at times information must be discussed slowly and then repeated. You can be sure that the doctor would want the same courtesy if his or her child were hospitalized. When talking to the doctor about your complaints, be specific. Rely on your notes. The doctor may not be aware of procedures in his or her own hospital, or your complaint may be similar to others the doctor has received in the past.

REMEMBER: The doctor's primary concern is to care for your child. If you have legitimate complaints about the care the child is receiving, the doctor will want to hear them.

At times you may only have to speak to the head nurse. The head nurse should be interested in how the floor functions. The head nurse should be able to correct deficiencies in the hospital care given your child or at least provide you with an adequate explanation. Sometimes you may have to discuss the matter with both the head nurse and the doctor. Open discussion should convey to both the head nurse and the doctor that your primary concern is the care given your child.

If you are not happy with the care or the sequence of treatment, you may have to say to the hospital staff: "I don't think that Dr. R. would be happy with this." You could also say, "I don't think Dr. R. would go along with this." You may then have to ask: "Can this decision wait until we contact Dr. R?" Do not be afraid to say this even to a colleague of your child's doctor. Force the hospital staff members to explain their actions. If it appears that the hospital staff members are going to disregard your opinion or concern, you may have to say: "Dr. R was very specific about this. I'm sure she would want to be notified before you proceed." By now the hospital staff members should have gotten your message, and it should be clear to them that they had better check with the doctor.

Getting Ready for the Hospital

There are things you will want to do and know before your child is admitted to the hospital. If the child is admitted as an emergency case, preparation is very limited. If you and the child have time to prepare, you should consider the following:

Getting to know the hospital. Many hospitals have formal tours so that you and the child can become familiar with this new and different environment that will become the child's temporary home. By knowing ahead of time what to expect, you can reduce the number of unknowns for both you and the child. Sometimes, simply seeing where you will sleep, where you will eat, and where you may be operated on takes away some of the unnecessary anxiety. Often, the hospital staff showing you and the child around the hospital can anticipate possible concerns the child may have and answer those often unasked questions. By sharing the visit, you and the child can discuss things you saw together. Many times, the unknown is a lot worse than the real thing.

If the hospital you plan to use does not have a formal tour, ask your child's doctor to arrange for you to visit. By touring the hospital and having an opportunity to talk to the staff, you may be able to anticipate problems.

School. If your child is in the hospital for a long period of time, you should make arrangements to continue the child's schooling. Some children's hospitals have teachers who can carry on children's education in the hospital. Often, the school district will make arrangements for tutoring on a regular basis. Because school is part of a child's life and since your desire is to provide a structure within the hospital day for your child, you will want to arrange to bring the child's education to him or her. It is important to plan ahead of time with the hospital staff and with the school. When your child feels well enough to learn again, it is important to have an educational program ready. This will contribute to the child's sense of getting better.

Planning the Day. Initially, your child's hospital day will be filled with diagnostic tests, possible surgery, and the child's just not feeling well. But once this initial period is over, it is generally believed that the day is spent in the following manner:

10 hours asleep
 2 hours in treatment
12 hours free time

The largest block consists of twelve hours of unused time. Try to plan ahead by bringing materials to the hospital that will occupy the child's time. These do not have to be expensive items. Television is probably the most time-occupying event for a sick child. You may want to find out ahead of time whether the hospital has a television rental service, how much it costs, and whether you can bring a television from home. Many general hospitals also provide child life workers (formerly called play ladies), who are hired by the hospital to plan events that children on pediatric floors can become involved with on a daily basis. Rather than having your child lie in bed and recuperate, it is better that the child become involved in activities that encourage independence and health.

Parents, take care of thyself. Along with preparation that will make your child's stay at the hospital easier, it is important that you take care of your own needs. By using family and close friends appropriately, you can set up a network of relief rather than continuously staying in the hospital. It is important to the nonhospitalized members of your family that you maintain involvement with them and continue to play as much a part in their daily lives as you can. If you set up a predictable daily schedule, even the very youngest children can accept your temporary absence. This is particularly true when the child is hospitalized for a long period.

Food. Hospital food is notoriously bad. While touring the hospital, find out its policy on food. Unless your child needs special foods, there may be no medical reason why you cannot bring some meals from home. Even children with special diets may find it more tasteful if supplemented by foods from outside the hospital that still meet their medical requirements. Complaining about the food sometimes helps. Often you can speak with the dietician who supervises the floor on which your child is hospitalized. It should be possible for your child, if he or she is medically well enough, to eat with other children. The message to a child who is allowed to eat out of bed is far more encouraging than the message that the child is still sick enough to have to eat in bed.

Going Home
Some time before the child is discharged from the hospital, you will want to plan for it. Getting out of the hospital usually is a very happy and exciting time. Unnecessary delays can be avoided by planning ahead of time. It is important that you discuss with the

doctor the progress he or she expects your child to make after discharge from the hospital. This will give you some idea about the course of recuperation and provide you with a schedule for recuperation. If your child's schedule for getting well doesn't follow the expected course, you will know that the doctor must be contacted.

You may have to know how to care for the child after discharge from the hospital. In many cases, children are not fully recovered from either the illness or the surgery that brought about the hospitalization. Although they do not need the specialized care of the hospital any more, they may still need nursing care at home. This may require changing bandages, giving medication, etc. Having observed the care your child received in the hospital, it should not be a shock or an unexpected demand when the doctor provides you with a list of care services the child may need. If you plan ahead of time, outside resources may be obtained should more specialized care be required, such as care provided by nurses, physical therapists, etc.

Another important aspect of the discharge is to discuss with your child and the doctor the various physical activities that the child can and cannot do. Involve your child in the planning, as this will allow the child to begin to regain independence. Many children become fearful of giving up the dependence they developed along with the attention they obtained while hospitalized. Making your child part of the discharge planning processes encourages this healthy change toward independence. Finally, discuss with the doctor what to do if you're worried and need to speak with him or her. Most likely, the doctor has an emergency call system as well as an office call system. It is not the same as meeting the doctor each day in the hospital, but the need is not as critical.

POINTS TO REMEMBER

1. *The daily structure.* The best way to ensure that your child "survives" a hospital stay with the fewest crises is to develop a daily structure. In this way, you, your child, and the doctor plan for each day, and any deviations are immediately recognized, discussed, checked, and corrected if necessary. Since all children seem to thrive better within a clearly defined and structured

environment, it makes sense to try to provide a structure to the hospital day. In doing this, you will help the hospital staff as well as the doctor know how to communicate with you and thus inform them of what you and your child expect of them.

2. *General versus children's hospital.* Children's hospitals have been developed to provide a special setting for the care of the sick child. These hospitals tend to have highly specialized medical and nursing care for children. However, such hospitals tend to be few and far apart. General hospitals can be differentiated by their attitude toward your child and toward you. The crucial difference may simply be that some general hospitals encourage your participation whereas other hospitals tolerate it. Obviously, you will want your child hospitalized where your participation is encouraged actively.

3. *The ally.* As in the case of the emergency room, it is important that you identify an ally among the hospital staff. This person should be at the highest level of competency, thus lending some authority to the information being shared with you. This may be the head nurse or an associate of the child's doctor. This person, being comfortable within the hospital setting, can provide additional answers to your questions and most likely will be more available to you than the doctor. Remember, the ally is not a substitute for the doctor. Rather, the ally complements the team caring for the child.

4. *Preparing your child and you.* It is very important that you and your child familiarize yourselves with the hospital the child will enter. This facilitates discussion between you and the child and helps you both deal with your apprehensions. Reducing as much of the child's anxiety as is realistically possible will not only make the hospitalization less traumatic but will encourage recuperation.

The Dentist

Your child will need dental care throughout his or her life. The dental care received during early childhood and adolescence will greatly influence dental health throughout the child's life. Too often parents make the mistake of believing that because a dental problem is affecting only "baby teeth," care is not necessary. It follows the myth that since baby teeth are only temporary, the quality of care provided them should be neither as involved nor as good as the care provided for "permanent" teeth. Yet in many instances, adult teeth are directly influenced by baby teeth in terms of placement and quality. Your child's mouth can become a center for many problems associated with poor oral hygiene. Often, poor dental care can lead to prolonged and painful treatment of an oral condition that good and early intervention could have avoided.

Your child will need a personal dentist. This dentist may be the same person you use for care of your teeth and mouth. You should consider using a pedodontist, a dentist who specializes in children. A pedodontist has had specific training in caring for the teeth and mouths of children. Since pedodontists spend a great deal of time working with children, they probably are more comfortable dealing with the emotional traumas and reactions of children that are associated with seeing a dentist. A pedodontist is more likely to have seen very young children (under the age of five) so that he, his staff, and his office are better prepared to handle your child in the least offensive and traumatic way.

A General Dentist or a Pedodontist?

In choosing between a general practice dentist and a pedodontist, consider that a general dentist may not be comfortable treating very young children. Age is an important factor to take into consideration when deciding when your child should start visiting a dentist. The pedodontist has both the staff and the equipment for dealing with children, thus making the experience as pleasant as possible under the circumstances. Given the right person for your child, a visit to the dentist can be less traumatic for the child than for you. A general dentist's practice involves mostly adults. The staff and office are not specifically set up for children. This is not to say that such a dentist cannot treat your child adequately. You may feel very comfortable using your own dentist for your child, realizing that he or she will make referrals should your child need special interventions (root canal work, etc.). It is also very possible that a pedodontist is not conveniently located near you or that none practices in your community. These circumstances may force you to make certain choices. However, given the general infrequency of visiting the dentist, a pedodontist is your child's best bet.

Picking the Dentist

Your child's dentist will be picked in much the same way you picked the pediatrician. The methods for choosing are identical: inheritance, reputation, and recommendation. The inheritance method works in this manner: "I use this dentist for myself, and so I will use him for my child." In this case, your child will receive initial care from a general dentist. The reputation method relies on word of mouth from friends, neighbors, and relatives. This is probably the most common method, and often the child will end up in a pedodontist's office. If you talk with individuals who are pleased with the dental care that their children receive and you feel that these individuals would expect and demand the same high standards that you would want for your child, you will be comfortable with that choice. Be careful of the dentist whose reputation is based on the fact that he or she is inexpensive. Choosing your child's dentist on the basis of price may cost the child more in the long run.

The recommendation method involves asking the child's pediatrician or other trained professionals. The pediatrician should have a dentist (or dentists) in mind not only for the children he cares for but also for his own children. Other recommendations for a dentist can be gathered by calling a dental school if there is one in your community or city, checking with the American Dental Association Directory, calling the local dental association, or even calling the general hospital in your community, which may have accredited dental services associated with the hospital.

Whatever the method used, it is very important to have a dentist chosen for your child before he or she needs one. This means choosing the dentist somewhere before the child's third birthday, when all teeth should be in (baby teeth) and the child should be mature enough to cooperate with the dentist. The dentist will have to watch the growth and health of not only your child's teeth but his or her oral cavity (mouth).

The First Visit

Before the first visit, it is very important that you prepare your child for the dentist. For the very young child (preschool age), preparation is limited. Beyond that age, most children are aware of dentists and their role. Schools usually spend time providing information about the role of a dentist and the care of teeth. Most children are aware that they will have to see a dentist. In setting up the first appointment, discuss with the receptionist how you might prepare your child for the visit. If you can speak directly with the dentist, he or she should be able to help.

The first visit should be preparatory; it should be used to familiarize your child with the dentist, the office, and some of the dental interventions the child may need in the future. This is the time when the dentist explains some of the things that will be done to your child and the use of some of the instruments. Although this appointment may not accomplish anything in a corrective sense, it will familiarize the child with, and reduce potential anxiety about, interventions in future dental care. This first visit provides a smoother transition for the child who requires dental care and makes the whole experience less traumatic.

If the first appointment is set up with your own general dentist, it is important that you speak with the dentist directly. If you are setting up the appointment with the receptionist, ask to speak with the dentist by saying: "I would like to speak with Dr. J. about how she will treat my child." The dentist, especially if you use him or her as a general dentist, will want to speak with you. If he or she doesn't, you may have to reconsider your choice.

In speaking with the dentist before the first visit, you will want to find out if the dentist does the following:

• *Space maintenance.* This includes care of the child's teeth so that mature teeth replacing baby teeth are not displaced.
• *Pulpotomies.* This is a fancy name for root canals. Even children's teeth may require root canals rather than extraction.
• *Crowns.* Often a child needs crown work (metal coverings over a tooth, such as in the case of a molar). This is complicated and difficult in children but is often necessary.

After you have asked the above questions, you will want to ask the following: "Are these procedures something you do often?" If the dentist's reply gives you a sense that he or she is comfortable with these procedures, you will want to set up an appointment.

REMEMBER: Find out how much the dentist will charge. Good dental care can be financially prohibitive. Ask the dentist what kind of plans he or she has for paying off the child's dental costs over time.

Once you have arranged for the child's dental appointment, ask the dentist: "What should I tell my child about coming to the dentist?" The dentist should be able to help you prepare the child and can give you some words that will help the child understand what to expect. The dentist's response to this can give you some idea how he or she handles children, not only their dental needs but also their emotional needs.

Once at the Dentist's Office

Once you arrive at the dentist's office, you will want to check out the following:

1. *The office.* Is the waiting room child-oriented? As in a pediatrician's office, the dental waiting room should offer some distraction while your child waits. It should also be isolated from any activity or noise that may come from the examining room. What you are most concerned about is that the office provide your child with a comfortable environment.

2. *Handling your child.* Once again, it is important that your child be treated like a person. You may have to lead the way by treating and talking with the child as you would like others to do. The dentist should talk *to* your child, not *around* the child. If you feel that the dentist is not doing this, you should say: "My child understands more than you think and cooperates more when she understands what is going to happen to her." It is also important that the dentist use the right vocabulary when talking with your child. She may use descriptive words to explain what she will do ("sleepy juice" instead of needle, "wiggle a tooth out" instead of pull, "pinch" or "mosquito bite" instead of hurt).

3. *Parental involvement.* Ask the dentist whether you can be in the examining room when your child is being treated. Except for the very young child (under four years of age) or the extremely upset child, your presence is probably not necessary. If your child is extremely upset, the dentist should consider using sedation.

4. *Sedation and analgesics.* The dentist should be familiar with the various sedatives and analgesics so that your child has the least

offensive experience. In talking about analgesics, the dentist should not refer to them in terms of putting the child to sleep. Rather, the dentist should view analgesics as an aid to a novocaine injection (to deaden any pain) that helps distort time sensation so that the child is relaxed and cooperative. Nitrous oxide is often used in this situation. The dentist should also be familiar with behavior modification techniques. These techniques allow the dentist to relax and desensitize children to the various experiences they will be faced with. In most situations, a sensitive and clear approach by the dentist will be the most effective way of making this experience better.

5. *Prevention and diet.* It is important that the dentist help you and your child in the area of preventive measures and good diet. If the dentist does not talk with you about these two areas on your first visit, raise the question: "What are your feelings about prevention and diet in caring for teeth?" The dentist should offer you information about fluoride and its usefulness in preventing tooth decay. There are some who feel that regular cleaning of teeth and topical application of fluoride can decrease tooth decay by as much as eighty percent. A good general diet further helps in maintaining a healthy mouth.

6. *X-rays.* The dentist should be concerned about space maintenance and the ability of your child's mouth to accommodate emerging adult teeth. One way of evaluating this area is to take x-rays of the child's teeth. Many pedodontists have x-ray equipment that allows for a single x-ray of the entire mouth. The dentist should do this examination as a preliminary study of your child's possible need for orthodontic interventions.

REMEMBER: If your child needs orthodontic work, you will have to discuss this with the dentist. The orthodontist you use should be recommended by your child's dentist after a good preliminary orthodontic examination.

In talking with the dentist, there are many things you will want to know. Many of them will concern the comfort of the child while being treated. You should ask: "How uncomfortable will my child be while you work on her?" The dentist should talk about the use of novocaine to deaden the area to be worked on. Avoiding the use of novocaine is not always good, and many times the use of a pain deadener is preferred. The dentist should talk to you and your child about the "sleepy juice" (novocaine), how the rubber dam and irrigator (fluid collectors placed in the mouth) work, and protection from x-rays (lead shields). By discussing these matters with the dentist with your child present, you are doing two things. First, it lets the dentist know that you are interested not only in quality dental care but also in your child's comfort and protection. Second, it gives your child a sense that you will protect him or her from unnecessary discomfort.

Checklist for rating your child's dentist

☐ Respects your child and treats the child like a person

☐ Respects you, the parent

☐ Listens to you and the child patiently

☐ Puts you and the child at ease

☐ Explains things to the child and you so that you both understand them

There are two occasions that require special attention: finding an orthodontist, and the dental emergency.

Finding an Orthodontist

Obviously, when considering an orthodontist, you will have to discuss the matter with the dentist. Since you feel that you made the proper choice in finding this dentist you will trust his or her opinion. If you have followed the recommendation of using a dentist as part of the child's general health care, the dentist will begin to share with you early in the child's growth and development concerns about teeth and proper placement. Once the decision is made that your child should be seen by an orthodontist, the process of finding one should follow the methods used for obtaining other services. You will rely on the inheritance, reputation, or recommendation methods. It is important in choosing an orthodontist that you realize that, like all professionals, they have various methods and goals concerning intervention. Since orthodontic work can be a costly endeavor, it is important that the objectives and goals, as well as the time and costs involved, be clearly defined before an agreement is signed (most orthodontists have you sign a contract for services). It would be very damaging to involve your child in an orthodontic plan, only to have to stop it halfway through because funds are no longer available. In discussing the matter with the dentist, see whether there are some interceptive steps that the dentist can do. The dentist should define for you where he or she draws the limits in the area of orthodontic intervention.

The Dental Emergency

The two most common dental emergencies for children involve toothache and trauma. The causes of toothache are many, ranging from an emerging adult tooth pushing out a baby tooth to advanced decay of an unhealthy tooth. Drugstore treatments seldom have value. Dental trauma usually implies breaking a tooth, most likely as a result of the child falling down or being hit. The dentist should have informed you how to reach him or her in case of an emergency. If the dentist is not available, the office should provide you with alternative treatment coverage, most likely through a covering dentist.

It is very important in a case of trauma that the child be seen by a pedodontist. Correct early treatment may save the child years of future problems, discomfort, and embarrassment. In the case of trauma, the child may need the services of an endodontist (a specialist in caring and treating the nerve roots of teeth) or an oral surgeon, who uses surgical interventions in the oral cavity and is trained to recognize and treat problems involving the jaw.

Should you and your child be out of town, you may need to find these services on an emergency basis. Such dental services may be found in the emergency room of the local hospital, which, if your child is fortunate enough, will have a pedodontist on staff. If not, you should ask: "Can my child be seen by a pediatric dentist?"

You may be advised of services outside of the hospital. If these are immediately available (have the emergency room call to see if your child can be seen), you will want to use them. There is usually a local dental society that can provide you with recognized pedodontists or general dentists who have advised the society that they are interested in the care of pediatric dental problems.

REMEMBER: You may want to obtain only an opinion from a new dentist. You should ask: "How soon do these interventions need to be done?" In this way, you can determine whether there is enough time for the child to see his or her own dentist. In many cases, temporary care can be provided, allowing you and the child to return to your usual dentist.

- Pick your child's dentist as part of the child's general health care.
- Know the difference between a pedodontist and a general dentist.
- Don't choose the cheapest and don't be overly impressed by the most expensive.
- Discuss with the dentist any discomfort your child may have while being cared for, and work with the dentist to reduce it.

REMEMBER: Your child is totally dependent on you for proper dental care. The dental care received as a child often will have a direct impact on the dental care the child will require as an adult.

Foods, Fads, and Additives

Providing your child with a healthy diet is no longer a simple matter. As a society, we rely almost entirely on others to provide us with food. Although homemade meals prepared with natural substances are being rediscovered, the fact remains that in the preparation of even basic staples, twentieth-century technology has altered our eating habits forever. That is not to imply that all the changes are for the worse. In the past we utilized organic substances to preserve foods we had to store. Today, this is done almost entirely with inorganic substances that are foreign to the human body. Your child is subjected to this additive intrusion on a daily basis. What effect it will have on the growing human body is unclear. Whether effects will be caused by exposure, accumulation, or both is unknown. Scientific study on the toxic as well as allergic effects of ingested substances is in its infancy.

Because there are two sides to every question, both sides must be looked at suspiciously. The food industry, by the simple fact that they must sell food and drink, will have a vested interest in supporting one side of the issue. Those who oppose junk food may overstate their case. As a parent protecting your child, you probably feel confused by all the declarations and statements. Simply stated, no one really knows what effect diet has on daily functioning or even on life span. The food industry, in order to meet the demands of a capricious public, must rely on many food additives to produce both variety and extended package life span (called "shelf life").

Unfortunately, it is a vicious cycle. Advertising, feeding on the whims of the ever-growing but always changing mind of your child, reinforces continued use of junk food. Your child in turn will want to have access to these advertised foods, regardless of their nutritional value or possible side effects. Today, the list of foods that are considered harmful to children is extensive. Such basic foods as apples, oranges, and strawberries are being looked at suspiciously. It has become increasingly important that parents have clear goals and objectives in determining the kind of food their children will eat. Expense, availability, and preparation time are considerations that force you to choose some foods over others. In considering diets, it is important that you view them in the following manner. In this way, your child will receive a sound and tasteful diet.

What Kind of Food Am I?

The misconceptions about foods are endless. What we have been led to believe is important to diet and health has at times been proved not only useless but harmful. If your child's diet consists of a balance of protein, carbohydrates, and vitamins (which are usually supplied through vegetables and fruits), the child is eating appropriately. With this knowledge, along with an understanding of your child's individual eating habits, tastes, and possible reactions to food, substitution in any one of the these three basic food classes is possible. When devising a diet for your child, it is important to decide what your overall goal is. Are you changing the child's diet for nutritional reasons alone? Do you have a therapeutic objective? Both?

Nutritional changes may be made not only in your child's diet but also for the entire family. The human body does not foresake its need for good food simply because it has reached a certain age. Therapeutic diets for children must be scrutinized closely. The number of therapeutic diets offered to parents in order to help their children is alarming because many of them are neither nutritionally sound nor therapeutic. Furthermore, their therapeutic claims remain scientifically untestable or are based on poor research. Some diets are viewed as being both nutritionally sound and as having therapeutic value. Although these diets may not live up to their therapeutic claims, they remain useful since they are nutritionally sound.

Therapeutic Diets

Therapeutic diets have been proposed, advertised, and criticized for years. The therapeutic value of certain foods and drinks has been postulated for centuries. The twentieth century has produced its own dietetic claimers. Most recently, diets such as the Feingold diet for hyperactive behavior have been touted. While the effects of some diets are made obvious by the reaction of your child to certain foods, others are not as clear. Hives and gastrointestinal reactions to certain foods dictate certain dietary changes. Such dietary changes are less reliable when used to treat headaches and disturbed behavior. In choosing a therapeutic diet for a child, it is important to keep in mind the following:

Overall Objectives. It is very important that you and your child (if old enough to participate) have a clear understanding of why the child is eating some foods and not others. The elimination of hives and diarrhea secondary to eating certain foods is more easily identified than a decrease in certain behaviors. Therapeutic diets are generally based on how a child reacts while on the diet as compared to when he or she was not on the diet. Obviously, a therapeutic claim can be made if the target symptoms disappear or the known reactions no longer occur (e.g. the child no longer gets hives). The measure of success for some of these diets, especially in dealing with behavioral symptoms, requires not just subjective impressions but objective criteria as well. For your child's sake, it is important that you use these measures so that the child and you are not led down some therapeutic yellow brick road, believing that something is working when it is not.

Scientific Research. A good therapeutic diet will withstand the critical eye of the researcher. Without adequate research, a child may be placed on a diet whose success is based on subjective rather than objective criteria. Many times, success is measured by parents reporting improvement to supporters of the diet. Unfortunately, parents and researchers are looking for success and tend to see improvement on the diet where there is none. At times, research and success with laboratory animals is translated into success with children.

REMEMBER: Children are not laboratory rats. The difficulty of doing good scientific studies in the area of diet and children is complicated by the number of different factors that have to be considered when you view any diet in relation to your child.

It is almost impossible to get a scientifically pure subject (no child lives in a vacuum or a scientifically controlled environment). Also, it is impossible to ensure that children used in studies, or even those under subjective scrutiny, maintain strict adherence to the recommended diets. Thus, monitoring infringements (nondietetic foods) is very difficult.

Another factor, used in almost all rigorous scientific research, is the placebo control. In this situation, the placebo control is a substitute that appears to be exactly the same as the diet food but includes the additives under observation. In this way, your child would try food that looked and tasted exactly like the diet food, except that it would also include the "bad" substances removed by the diet. This would allow for a more scientific comparison. Without such research, you might react to your child differently, believing that the diet you chose was working. In this way, you are changing not just the child's diet but also your interactions with the child (which may be a more positive reinforcer for changing behavior in the child). Finally, the reintroduction into the diet of the offending dietary substances does not always lead to a clear reoccurrence of the negative symptoms or behaviors. What does all this mean for your child? The final results (scientific) and conclusions are still not in for the therapeutic claims of many of these diets. That is not to say that there won't be positive findings in the end, but for now the claims made by diet supporters remain inconclusive.

Psychological Considerations. It is important to remember that your child is subjected to a world that may have little concern about what the child eats or drinks as long as it tastes good. This world includes the school cafeteria (discussed elsewhere in this book), the corner store, the shopping center, and friends' houses. While we as adults may have the maturity to deny ourselves dietary pleasures because they may be harmful to our bodies, it is unreasonable to ask that of children. It is important, then, to consider the psychological effects on any child who is segregated and isolated by diet. The younger the child, the less likely that the child will want to lose anonymity from his or her peers because of a diet. Children do not like having a finger pointed at them because they are made to eat certain kinds of foods. Furthermore, they need to learn how to refuse foods offered them that others do not see as being harmful. Some explanations that your child can use are easier than others. Refusal because "I'm allergic to milk" is more acceptable to the general public and peers than refusing bubble gum because "I get 'hyper' when I eat it."

Any diet must be explained carefully and some explanations are more easily understood than others. Your child will need help in learning what to say to others (e.g., peers or other parents) when refusing certain foods. Certainly, it is important that you discuss your child's dietary needs with those who come in contact with the child. This may require calling the school cafeteria manager, the teacher (they have a lot of parties in the classroom), and friends' parents (if the child spends time in their houses and sometimes eats there). All these calls make it easier for the child to accept dietary restrictions. It is also important to talk with the child about how he or she feels about not eating certain foods that other children eat all the time. By saying, "It's very hard not to eat candy," you can elicit the child's feelings about reactions to the eliminated foods. I have been impressed by the number of children placed on therapeutic diets who have become increasingly angry and thus "acted out" as a result of feeling different.

Cost. Some diets are expensive. Given the lack of scientific research to back up their therapeutic claims, the cost can be even greater. Some diets are of the inclusive kind, requiring substances to be added to the diet. Some children require special diets because of health problems (such as the diabetic child). The cost of these diets is easily understood. The cost of diets of questionable therapeutic value needs to be weighed more carefully.

Talking to Other Parents. Before considering a diet, especially one that is therapeutic, talk with other parents whose children are on a similar diet.

REMEMBER: These parents may have accepted the diet for their child without the same degree of scrutiny that you are applying to the same diet before accepting it for your child.

Ask the following questions:

• "Who told you about this diet?" It is important and useful to find out how another parent learned about a diet. Often, they have learned about it through a pediatrician or organization that may have either scientific research or past experience to back up their claims. Remember to take down names, since it may be useful to you on occasion to get in touch with these sources.

• "Why was your child placed on the diet?" This can be a comforting question in that you may find that your child is not the only one suffering from food reactions. It is also important because the specific target symptoms you wish to eliminate through diet may be exactly the same ones the parent with whom you are talking also wanted to eliminate. You can then ask specific questions about those symptoms.

• "Did you read any scientific papers about the diet?" It is hoped that this parent will have done some research before placing his or her child on any diet. If the parent has tried to find supportive data, he or she can share with you not only the material but the conclusions. The absence of research information is also important.

• "How has your child reacted to the diet?" Finding out the reactions of another child may help you to understand better your child's possible reactions. Did the target symptoms disappear or are they the same? Maybe there were side benefits from the diet not originally expected. This could be reason enough for you to use the diet for your child. What were the emotional effects of the diet?

• "What are some of the problems in keeping your child on the diet?" This question is very useful in that it helps you prepare yourself and your child better for potential pitfalls while the child is on the diet. If the child doesn't like the diet, this may help you know what to look for in terms of food indiscretions (cheating on the diet).

• "Is it difficult to maintain the diet on a daily basis?" It is very nice to use a diet if in fact you and your child can apply it in the community. Some diets require unusual foods, substitutions, or additions that may not be readily available. If you cannot stick to a diet, it will not have the desired effects and thus will not fulfill its stated purpose.

● "How long did your child have to stay on the diet before it worked?" While your child may not respond to the diet in the same way as any other child, it is useful to have some idea of a time schedule. This can also be shared with your child. Some diets require longer trial periods than others.

REMEMBER: In some cases, it is important that certain substances be eliminated from the body entirely. This may require weeks.

This section is not meant to be an in-depth discussion of nutrition and diets. Many other books are readily available. But it is very important that you be able to scrutinize your child's eating habits. In this way, you can ensure the child's continued growth and development. There are competitive forces that your child encounters on a daily basis whose interests in what your child eats are not the same as yours. For them, the motivation for having your child eat certain foods is to make money, sell an idea, or support a claim. Since the food industry is very large and very persuasive, it remains up to you to protect your child. It is also up to you to protect the child against the therapeutic claims of certain diets until they are supported by rigorous scientific research. Nothing should be accepted at face value.

POINTS TO REMEMBER

● When deciding on a diet, do not forget the child's basic need for protein, carbohydrates, and vitamins.
● When deciding on a diet, are you choosing it for its nutritional value, therapeutic benefits, or both?
● When choosing a therapeutic diet, read the scientific research that backs it up (or doesn't).
● What effects does this diet have on your child other than the desired ones (e.g., psychological)?
● Is the diet practical? Cost? Availability?

• Diets that require elimination but maintain a balance (protein, carbohydrates, and vitamins) are more likely to be harmless than additive diets, even if their therapeutic claims turn out to be useless.
• Teenagers, especially girls, are prone to dieting in order to lose weight. Younger children who are seen as overweight are also often placed on diets. Weight-watching organizations are proliferating all over the country. Remember that your child needs to be followed closely by a pediatrician to monitor overall growth and development.

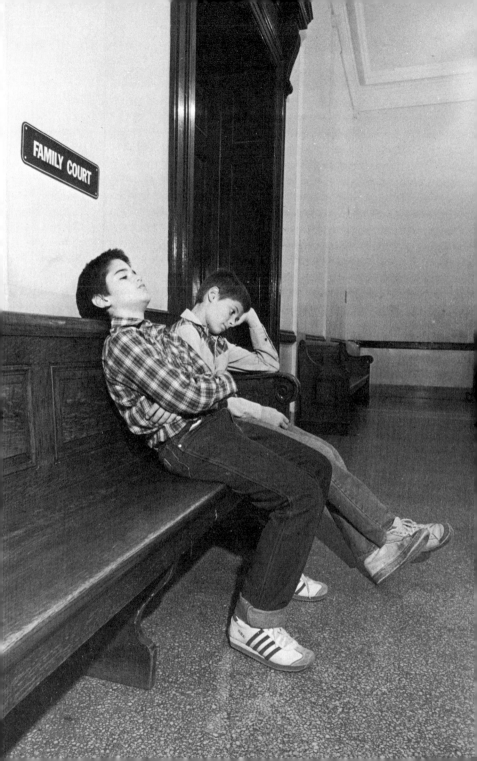

2

Legal Needs of Children

One day your child may need a lawyer. Most parents do not believe this and thus find themselves unprepared when the situation arises. The view that your child will need legal advice only if he or she commits a crime is misleading. Often there are other reasons for obtaining these services, but we will discuss only "crisis" legal services in this chapter.

Like the pediatrician or teacher, the lawyer can be another very important person in a child's life. Your child will most likely need a lawyer during a legal crisis that could have lasting impact on his or her future. Poor legal services have led to the improper guarding of many a child's rights.

As your child's guardian, it is important that you be aware of, although not an expert in, the child's legal rights and the proper boundaries within which others must operate. The first thing that will happen is that you will receive a phone call. It is likely to come from one of three sources: police, retail store, or school.

The Call

Initially, most parents are shocked by being called. This is only natural, especially if you have had no reason to be concerned about your child's behavior. The initial call is a very important time. You must not panic. You have to respond carefully, thoughtfully, and forcefully. You should do the following:

1. Ask the name of the person with whom you are speaking and his or her position (unless you already know the person, such as a school official). Ask the person to repeat his or her name, stating, "Please repeat that so I can write it down." This begins the *statement fact sheet*, which is a written account of your child's detainment, including names, statements, and any other pertinent information.
2. Ask the person calling, "Are you in charge?"
3. Ask the person calling to be specific about what happened and to tell you whether there are any charges. Don't settle for the statement "We will discuss that once you get down here." It is very important that you know exactly what charges, if any, will be made against your child.
4. Ask the person calling, "Who made the charges?"
5. Ask the person calling, "How long has my child been detained?"

REMEMBER: Write all this information down and let the person with whom you are speaking know that you are taking notes. Ask that person to repeat information for your statement fact sheet by stating, "Would you please repeat that, as I am writing it down."

6. Ask the person, "What was my child's reaction?" This will give you some idea of how the child is handling the situation. Some children will be very upset and tearful, while others (probably equally as frightened) may put on a "cool" front. The person detaining your child, if he or she has had experience with children, will see through the cool outside, and this will help you determine something about the sensitivity of this person.
7. Ask the person calling, "May I speak with my child?" This is very important. You must, however, obtain the above information first. If the person calling answers no, say, "I don't understand why you're preventing me from speaking with my child. What is the *regulation* or *rule* that forbids my talking with her, as I wish to note it down."

8. When you speak to your child, your initial reaction may be to beat the child up over the phone. That would be very destructive. Reassure the child that you will be coming shortly. Advise the child not to discuss the matter further or sign any document. Then ask to speak with the person who called. Tell that person, "I've advised my child not to discuss this matter further until I arrive." This lets that person know that the child's refusal to discuss the matter further is the result of your directive. In this way, he or she will not see this refusal as the child's way of being a wise guy.

9. Your final statement to the person detaining your child should be: "As soon as I hang up the telephone, I will be speaking with my child's lawyer." This is absolutely necessary, especially if in step 8 they do not let you talk to the child.

Calling the Lawyer

After you have received the initial call and have gathered the information on a statement fact sheet, you will have to find a lawyer for the child. Although different situations call for different lawyers, the matter about which you received the call, a crisis, will usually prevent you initially from getting the exact lawyer you need. Pick a lawyer for your child in much the same way you have found other professionals to provide services. The methods used are inheritance, recommendation, and "out of the blue."

The inheritance method is the result of the family having a lawyer whom they have used previously. Often, this lawyer has made out the family will or helped you buy a house. It is important that you know and trust the lawyer and that he or she can give you some immediate legal advice. It is not important that the lawyer be an expert in matters pertaining to youthful offenders, but you must trust the lawyer.

The recommendation method is the result of calling a friend, a relative, or possibly the family lawyer to get the name of either a family lawyer or a lawyer who is experienced in matters pertaining to juveniles.

The "out of the blue" method is the result of having neither of the above options and using either the local bar association to give you a name or looking up a lawyer in the telephone book. This may be the case if you are out of town and do not have access to any other information. You may want to call home to your family lawyer and obtain a recommendation over the phone. If that is not possible, lawyers are now advertising their services, and you may be able to determine those who have experience with juveniles. Obviously, this method of choosing a lawyer requires that you be able to ask the proper questions to determine whether the lawyer is both competent and trustworthy. (These questions are discussed later in this section.)

Once you have the name of a lawyer, you will have to call. Usually, you will talk first with the secretary. Immediately, let the secretary know that the situation is a crisis, that your child is being detained or has been arrested, and that you need immediate legal advice. Once the lawyer is on the phone, you must do the following:

1. Explain the situation. Be specific. Remember to use the notes that you collected on the statement fact sheet. The lawyer should also be taking notes, and you can say, "Do you want me to repeat anything so that you can note it down?" This will also give you an idea as to whether this is the appropriate lawyer for your child.

2. Once you have given the facts of the situation, ask the lawyer directly: "Is this the type of case you handle?" The lawyer should answer you honestly and directly. If he or she hesitates, ask, "If you prefer not to handle this matter, can you recommend someone who will?" The lawyer may respond by stating that this is not his or her kind of case and then recommend another lawyer.

3. At this point, if the lawyer has agreed to work with you, ask what steps come next. It is helpful to determine whether a call from the lawyer would be appropriate. Such a call can have a very strong effect. It notifies the people who have detained your child that the process they plan on carrying out will be monitored closely by a professional.

4. You and the lawyer need to clarify what your mutual goals are, for instance, that you want the child released into your custody. The lawyer should talk to you about possible options; if not, ask

the lawyer to explain them to you. It is very important that the lawyer and you agree beforehand on a course of action.

5. The lawyer should suggest that after calling the person detaining your child, he or she will also speak to the child and let the child know that he or she is now the child's lawyer. (This is important in determining whether the lawyer will see your child as a client and develop a relationship with the child.)

6. At this point, you will discuss with the lawyer the proper actions to take when you go to see your child and the people detaining the child. You should discuss setting up any necessary appointments with the lawyer.

7. One final but important point must be made. The lawyer may advise you that it is not necessary to have a lawyer intervene. Discuss why the lawyer feels this way; if you are comfortable with that recommendation, you may wish to accept the lawyer's advice.

Picking Up Your Child

At a Police Station

When you arrive at the police station, it is very important that you think clearly. This may be difficult, given your surprise and possible disbelief. If after talking with your child on the phone you believe the child may have done something wrong, be sure to act in an appropriate manner. Even if the child has been accused falsely, how you handle yourself will help facilitate whatever steps need to take place. By the time you have arrived at the police station, the lawyer should have called and obtained the following information:

1. The charges and circumstances under which the child was detained. These charges should match up with the information you obtained on the statement fact sheet.

2. Whether the matter is going to be processed, and if so, whether it will be processed as a criminal matter.

REMEMBER: If charges are not dropped, your child will be booked. That means basic information on an official record.

3. If bail is necessary and obtainable, the lawyer will discuss the release of your child to your custody after arranging for these matters.

Your primary goal is to take your child home. As a parent, you need to do the following:

1. Talk to the child alone. You can be adamant about this. Although the police may want to talk to you first, tell them that there will be plenty of time to talk after you have seen that your child is all right. Although you may be very angry, this is not the time to berate the child. It is very important that you find out the circumstances under which the child was detained. See whether these facts match up with the information you gathered on the statement fact sheet. Ask what your child has said and whether he or she signed any papers. This is very important. Having talked with your child, you can talk to the police.
2. Ask the police again the circumstances under which the child was detained. Again, match these facts against the facts given to you over the phone. If the information doesn't match up, ask the person you're speaking with to repeat his or her statement, saying: "This information doesn't match up with what I was told over the phone." Give the name of the person with whom you spoke.
3. If at this point charges will be dropped, you have only to take the child home. If, however, charges are not going to be dropped, the lawyer should have arranged for your child's release.
4. If your child signed a statement, ask to have a copy of it. If the police refuse for any reason, say, "I would like to read it, and I will make a copy of it myself, by hand if necessary."
5. At this point, advise the police that you and your child will not discuss the matter further without your lawyer present. Do this in a polite manner. If the police insist that there are more questions, say, "If you insist on more questions, you will have to call my attorney first."

The seriousness of the charges against your child and whether charges will be dropped will determine any immediate and further contact with the lawyer. If the child is booked (fingerprinted and charges filed), contact the child's lawyer, who will discuss with you the next steps to be taken.

At a Retail Store

Children of all ages can be detained in stores. Most often it is because they are believed to have been involved in shoplifting. When you arrive at the store, you must follow many of the steps outlined for the police station. The major difference is that the police probably have not been called yet and formal charges probably have not been made. You should, however, call your lawyer and have him or her call the store. By the time you arrive, if the lawyer has called, it is possible that the store and the lawyer have settled the matter.

If the matter has not been settled, it is very important that you talk to the child alone and again hear the circumstances under which he or she was detained. If the child admits to the charges, it may be important to ask the person detaining the child the following question: "If my child did what you charge her with, what would you want at this time?"

Basically, you are negotiating on behalf of the child. If payment (compensation) is what the stores desires, you may pay for the merchandise taken and your child will be allowed to leave. This is done with the understanding that all charges are dropped and no further action will be taken. If the store desires to press charges, you will have to wait for the arrival of the police. *It is very important that you notify your child's lawyer.*

Again, it is important that you remember the following:

1. *You have your statement fact sheet.* Ask the person detaining your child to repeat the allegations so that you can compare the two stories.
2. *Find out the exact status of the person you are dealing with,* making sure you have the correct name and the name of the immediate supervisor. You may want to ask: "Have you contacted your supervisor in this matter?" If the person replies that he or she hasn't, you should ask, "Why not?" This may force the person to call the immediate supervisor and be told by that person that he or she may be pursuing a course of action that the store would rather avoid.
3. *If your child has signed any statement,* ask the circumstances under which the statement was signed and whether you can have a copy of it. If they will not give you a copy, ask to see the statement and make a handwritten copy of it yourself.

At the School

Because schools can take disciplinary action against your child without involving the police, it is very important that when you arrive at school and talk to the person detaining your child you specifically ask:

1. "Please repeat the allegations you have made against my child." You will compare them with the statement fact sheet.
2. "What are your immediate plans concerning this matter?"
3. If the school plans on following through with the charges but not involving the police, find out specifically who they are going to have at the "hearing" and what the specific consequences (disciplinary action to be taken) will be if your child is found guilty.
4. Ask the person detaining your child whom he or she has discussed this matter with (e.g., principal or superintendent of schools).
5. Ask the person detaining your child to put all charges and allegations in writing so that you can compare them with your statement fact sheet.

At this time, you should do the following:

1. State, "I would hope that before you take action, you will give me a chance to talk with my attorney and go over the charges and allegations you will be sending me."
2. Request from the person detaining your child the specific education law under which charges will be filed.
3. Ask the person detaining your child: "Do you have to have a full hearing before taking action?" This notifies the person that action not taken at a formal hearing will be challenged. You will then ask, "Who will be at the full hearing?" Take down the names on the statement fact sheet.
4. If you know a member of your board of education, you will want to say: "I will discuss the procedure with Mr. or Mrs. R. as a member of the board of education." This allows the person detaining your child to know that the matter must be handled in a proper manner.
5. Before you agree to any informal or formal hearing, inform the person detaining your child that you need to discuss the matter with the child's lawyer. Never go before any hearing without your child's lawyer unless the lawyer recommends it.

If the school decides that the matter requires the police, you will have to follow the steps outlined for the police station.

REMEMBER: The purpose is not to determine the guilt or innocence of your child at this time but to ensure that the child's rights are guarded and that those detaining the child realize that you will do *whatever* is necessary to make sure that the matter is handled in a proper manner.

Meeting With the Lawyer

Once you have brought your child home, you will discuss the circumstances under which the charges and allegations were made. An appointment will have been made to meet with the child's lawyer. If you continue to work with the inherited lawyer, you will have much of the basic information you need to know. It is good practice to discuss the following matters with the lawyer:

1. *Fees.* Find out how much time the lawyer thinks he or she will have to devote to the case and the fee that will be charged. Although many lawyers charge by the hour, you may want to work out a contract fee (a fee not based on hourly rates). If this fee seems high, compare it with the number of hours you think will be devoted by the lawyer to the case and compute the costs. Remember, as in all other services, that a higher price does not mean better service.
2. *Past experience.* Again ask the lawyer what his or her experience has been in cases like your child's.
3. *Provider of service.* Ask specifically, especially if the lawyer is in a partnership, whether the lawyer will handle the case personally. If you are paying for the lawyer's services, you don't want someone else doing the work. Let the lawyer know that you will not be comfortable if someone else handles the case without your consent.
4. *Criminal cases.* If the case against your child is handled as a criminal matter, you need to know what experience the lawyer has had in criminal trial work. You may have to make inquiries about the lawyer's reputation in this field.

The following is a checklist when evaluating your child's lawyer:

☐ Does the lawyer take enough time with you or do you feel rushed?

☐ Do you feel you understand what the lawyer is saying to you and that the lawyer answers your questions patiently? If you don't understand, say to the lawyer: "I don't understand what you are saying," or "Would you explain that again so that I can understand it?" Remember, you will be taking information down on your statement fact sheet.

☐ Does the lawyer ask to talk to your child alone (especially if the child is an adolescent)? Do not perceive this private talk as a threat to your authority. You can ask what was discussed, but you may not be told. Furthermore, you may not need to know. It is important that the lawyer treat your child with respect and honesty.

☐ After you have discussed the situation, ask the lawyer: "Are you comfortable doing this kind of work or trial?" Does the lawyer hesitate? If so, suggest that you would be willing to pay for the services of anyone the lawyer thinks might be helpful. You can ask, "Is there someone you can work with who would be helpful in this matter?"

☐ Does the lawyer, as the case is discussed, refer to community services or agencies involved with juveniles? This will give you some additional information about the lawyer's involvement with juvenile cases.

If you are dissatisfied, you must discuss this with the lawyer. You can do this by saying: "I'm having difficulty communicating and understanding what you are saying. Since it is very important that we are able to talk to each other, we need to understand each other." If the lawyer becomes defensive and misses the point, you may have to consider obtaining the services of a new lawyer.

In communicating with the lawyer, it is important that you can call if you have a question. You will need to ask: "Is it all right if I call you?" If you are calling, ask "Am I calling too much?" This allows for you and the lawyer to set up some rules of communication. Always make sure you write down your questions before making the call. These questions and the lawyer's answers become part of the statement fact sheet.

What to Know About Family Court
if Your Child Needs To Go

Should charges be pressed against your child, most likely they will be done in family court (the usual age limit is sixteen). It is very important that the lawyer go over with you and your child exactly what to expect in the courtroom. The procedure in family court is different from most other courtroom proceedings in that it tends to be more informal. The informality of the proceedings is intentional; it allows for a greater latitude and participation among all the individuals involved. It is the responsibility of the lawyer to give you and your child a running account of what to expect ahead of time. The lawyer should, in a sense, carry out a "mock trial" so that you and the child will be familiar with the proceedings, the possible actions and ways the judge may handle various situations, and the language of the courtroom. The language of the courtroom can affect your child's case. How questions are answered becomes extremely important at times. Many times, despite the informality, questioning can become intense and tricky, and the situation can be tense.

There are specific things you and your child can do beforehand to prepare yourself for court.

1. *Bring a pad and pencil.* This allows you and the child the chance to take notes and send messages to each other and to the lawyer. Remember, you will have a statement fact sheet with you, and the story being told before the court may not correspond to the facts you obtained. The lawyer will want to know about any discrepancies as soon as possible.
2. *Talk to the lawyer in the courtroom.* It is important that you find out ahead of time how you can talk to the lawyer during the proceedings. A written question or statement to the lawyer may not be sufficient, and you will need to know the proper time to talk.
3. *Ask the court to be heard.* There are certain times when you can ask the court to be heard. This is different from other courtroom proceedings and reflects the latitude and informality of the family court process. You may wish to correct a fact that has been presented to the court or make a statement. Furthermore, the lawyer may wish for you to be heard by the court. Often, you

or your child can talk in a courtroom in a very different manner than a lawyer. (Lawyers are usually bound by rules that do not apply to clients.)

4. *Know who is in the courtroom.* Because family court is a private procedure, you can request to know which individuals will be in the courtroom. You and your child have a right to request that anyone not directly related to the case be denied access.

It is important to remember that family court records of your child can be removed, but only if the charges are dismissed or dropped. Otherwise, the trial record and booking procedures remain part of a permanent record. These records are not public information and *usually* are permanently sealed.

Other Things to Know

• *Teaching the child a lesson.* Sometimes, especially with older adolescents, there is value in not acting too quickly. The consequences of one's behavior are sometimes best taught by allowing the processes of society to take their course of action (e.g., allowing your child to go to trial). What is important is that no one's rights be denied through ignorance.

• *Creative sentencing.* At times, in order to get help for your child (e.g., psychiatric services that you may not be able to afford or that the child has resisted in the past), the family court process can help you. This can be arranged by using and working with the lawyer and in turn with the family court judge.

• *Plea bargaining.* Although most people are aware that plea bargaining occurs with adults, it is also practiced in the family court. Traditionally, this practice has allowed defendants to plead guilty to a lesser charge without a trial and thus avoid the possibility of being found guilty of a more serious charge. If your child confesses to you that he or she is guilty of the charges, discuss plea bargaining with the lawyer.

• *Talk beforehand.* In much the same way as in sex education, you should discuss ahead of time with your child how to react should the child be detained. As you have read, the initial contacts with those detaining your child may be the most important. Knowing some of the rules of the game will make it less traumatic for all involved.

• Discuss ahead of time what your child should do if he or she is detained. Prepare some responses so that the child is both cooperative and assertive, recognizing that the child will be very nervous should such a situation arise.

• From the initial call, begin to compile your statement fact sheet. It should be a running account of what people say and who says what. It is essential when there are contradictions of fact.

• You have to have trust in your child's lawyer. If greater expertise is necessary, your relationship with the lawyer should allow you to ask and for the lawyer to obtain any necessary additional resources.

• Always ask yourself: "Do I understand what is being said, what is happening, and what will happen next?" If you don't, start asking questions.

• Your child should feel that he or she can work with the lawyer. If your child can't, it is very important to discuss this openly, even with the lawyer present.

• Be aware of any formal hearing or proceedings beforehand. Ask as many questions as necessary before stepping into a courtroom or formal hearing so that you and your child have some idea of what to expect.

Action words to remember are *detained and arrested, statement fact sheet, names of people, "I've advised my child," lawyer, regulations,* and *experience in this kind of case.*

Review of Situations Where You Use the Action Words

• *Detained and arrested.* These two words are useful in getting through to the lawyer. The receptionist may have to hear from you: "I need immediate help as my child is being detained," or "My child has been arrested."

• *Statement fact sheet.* From the point of the initial call, let any person you are talking with know that you are taking notes. This notifies the person that you will be able to read from your notes any contradictions in information that person may have given you. You are less apt to be challenged if you have written information as opposed to information you are recalling from memory. Say the following: "Would you repeat what you have just said so that I can check my notes?" When you go to the place where the child is being detained, make sure you continue to take notes (names and copies of any documents) so that you have a comparison record for the future.

• *Names of people.* Always ask the person with whom you are talking for his or her name, position, and role in the case. People who have to identify themselves and realize that what they say will be attributed to them are more careful about what they say and attempt to do.

• *"I've advised my child."* This is a very important statement to make to any person detaining your child. It removes any burden from the child to answer further questions and places the responsibility on you as the parent. Also, your child's refusal to talk or sign documents will not be misinterpreted as a sign of defiance.

• *Lawyer.* Overuse the lawyer's name and the fact that you cannot discuss anything or proceed further unless you have his or her professional advice. This is a reverse intimidation maneuver that can buy you time to think. It is also good common sense. Furthermore, it informs those detaining and dealing with your child that they will have to work within the rules of the system rather than trying to bend them to make a case.

• *Regulations.* At any point along the way, whether it is with your child's lawyer or with the person detaining the child, ask what regulations require them to act in any one specific manner or allow them to conduct themselves in such a manner. Don't be surprised if no such regulation exists.

• *Experience in this kind of case.* This is the most important question to ask so that you become comfortable with the lawyer and develop the necessary trust. Your child also has to feel that the lawyer knows what he or she is doing and will defend the child as well as possible. If you do not feel that the lawyer has the necessary expertise, you may have to switch lawyers.

3

Educational
Needs of Children

Your child spends thirty or more hours a week in a classroom with a teacher or teachers. During that time, the child is influenced in many ways. Not only is the child taught the lessons of reading, writing, and arithmetic, but through interaction with teachers, the child begins to develop strategies and methods for coping with the real world. The classroom is a place that can provide children with a chance to practice coping skills before entering the real world. Thus, the manner in which the teacher handles the child and the child's classmates is very important. The teacher's role in helping your child develop a good self-image and a sense of confidence is almost unique. Often the significance of this aspect of the teacher's role is overlooked because some teachers fail to see the direct relationship between learning and high self-esteem.

The classroom provides one of the environments for the transition from early childhood to young adulthood. No other institution will have as much influence on the average child as the school. Its importance is further magnified by its effect on children during their critical developmental years. Within this environment, moral values and ethical choices will be influenced. The occupational choice your child makes may be heavily swayed by a single teacher or by exposure to a single learning experience. For the elementary school-age child, the foundation for successful achievement and the development of a positive self-image start with success in the classroom. A single negative classroom experience can have a devastating impact on the young and impressionable elementary school child. A constrictive and repressive learning environment can forever turn off the emerging adolescent.

Teachers can have long-lasting effects on a child. Elementary school-age children usually come in contact with only one or possibly two teachers on a regular basis. This is not the case at the middle school (formerly known as junior high school) or high school level, where the child comes in contact with many teachers. Teachers create learning experiences. These experiences can be positive or negative, and they reflect how central the teacher is to learning. The teacher's sensitivity to the fluctuating emotional, social, and cognitive needs of children is of the utmost importance. Many a teacher has "lost" a child by failing to be in tune with that child's changing needs for independence, creativity, and curiosity. The importance of finding the right teacher in the right classroom for your child is not restricted to the elementary school years. It continues on through high school.

In this section, you will learn how to find the right teacher for your child. To do this, you will need to know the following: what to look for, what to ask, whom to ask, when to ask, and what to do if you don't like what you see.

Before you start, remember that you must know your child before you match him or her with the right teacher in the right classroom. This takes into account not only what you believe about your child's ability but how the child deals in group situations and the kind of personality the child has. You must know whether your child requires clear structure and guidelines within which to learn, and you must know a teacher who can provide that structure. A child who is mature and has "inner" structure that can guide him or her through a variety of tasks without being constantly reminded would do better with a teacher who maintains less overt control over the learning process and uses independent work studies to facilitate learning.

It's important that you be honest with yourself about your child and the child's ability to learn. To fool yourself is to short-change your child. You begin learning about your child by communicating with nursery school and kindergarten teachers. They should share your child's experiences with you and help you understand the ways in which the child learns best. How your child learns may be more important than just knowing how much (IQ potential) the child can learn. When identifying the appropriate teacher, the most important fact may be the teacher's teaching style.

The Right School—The Right Teacher

Picking a school district is the first step in finding the right teacher. You may have this opportunity, since more families move every year. When you buy a house, ask the realtor about the school system. Tell the realtor that a good school district or a good local neighborhood school is a very important part of choosing where you will live. Realtors may not know about a specific school but usually have studied the situation because previous customers made schools an important part of their final decisions on housing.

Drive to the school to see how far away it is and to discover any transportation problems your child may have. Look at the outside of the school and the surrounding grounds (such as playgrounds). Nice-looking schools may not tell much about the quality of teaching, but they tell something about the community's interest and investment. A clean and orderly school tells your child how much the adults care about his or her education. A school with a run-down appearance tells your child that the adults around him won't make learning a priority investment.

If you are staying in a particular school district, you don't have the same latitude of choice as those who are moving. Families have moved from one school district to another, however, in order to provide their children with a better school environment. The next step is the same in either situation, except that those already living in a neighborhood have already begun the important process of asking around.

The method for finding a teacher for your child is similar to the method for obtaining other services. The best method is recommendation, which is done through asking around. Whether you are new in a school district or have been living there a while, you need to ask other parents about their experiences in a school and about the teachers. The following are essential questions for evaluating

a school. Keep in mind that your neighbors' recommendations may
be biased or inaccurate. By asking around enough, you will arrive
at an important consensus.

What to Ask About the School

• *How involved can parents become in the school?* A school with
a "closed door" policy does not want parental involvement. Without
such involvement, you will have a difficult time visiting classrooms,
talking with principals, and finding out through direct contact about
teachers. Although some schools will say that they are open to
parental involvement, they want that involvement in the form of
bake sales, fund raising, and other nonthreatening parental activities.

A school with an open door policy that attracts parental involvement through involving parents in some decision-making capacity
is a school that is amenable to change and constructive criticism.
For you and your child, this presents the best possibility for finding
the right teacher. Such schools see themselves as a part of the
community rather than *apart from* it and recognize the need to be
responsive to you and your child.

When questioning neighbors and friends, ask, "How are parents
involved in the school?" Try to get specific answers. Ask, "Were
you allowed to visit the classrooms unannounced or did you have
to make an appointment?" "Were parents involved on any commit-
tees looking at curriculum, discipline, etc.?"

• *What problems are there in communicating with the school?* Ask:
"Is there any policy that prevents you from calling a teacher directly
or do you have to go through the principal's office each time?" Ask:
"If I call the principal, how long does it usually take before the
principal returns my call?' (To wait over twenty-four hours is un-
acceptable unless the principal is involved in an emergency.)

• *What is teacher morale?* Ask: "How do you think the teachers
feel about the administration and the school?" Many times, parents
have learned indirectly or directly from teachers their attitude about
a school district, a principal, or the administration. Poor morale in
teachers can reduce the quality of teaching. Since your child can be
affected directly, this seemingly innocent question can reveal a great
deal.

• *How many field trips are there?* Ask: "How many field trips did your child take last year? Was that the usual number for her school or just for her class?" While field trips in and of themselves may not be the end-all in learning, they do indicate the attitude to learning experiences outside of the school. It is important not just how many field trips were made but whether their purpose is educational, recreational, or both.

What to Ask About the Teacher

You should ask the following questions of other parents about a teacher your child may have. It is important to remember that they may have had good and bad experiences with that teacher. Parents are not necessarily good observers, nor should they be expected to answer all of the following questions. If you ask a few parents, you can get a consensus. Later on in this section, you will be provided with additional ways to evaluate a teacher; by comparing that with what parents have said, you will arrive at your own opinion.

• *Can you communicate with the teacher?* Ask: "When you had a problem with your child related to school, how did you communicate with the teacher?" Although the teacher's ability to teach is very important, it is equally important to realize that learning occurs both at school and in the home. Problems that occur in one environment can affect the other. The importance of being able to talk and communicate with a teacher cannot be overstated. Ask: "When you call the teacher, does the teacher return your call the same day or later?" *A good teacher will want to know why a parent is calling.* While you may not expect an immediate phone call back, more than twenty-four hours is too long. Ask: "What is the teacher like on the telephone?" Does the teacher complain immediately about the class or your child, or does the teacher allow you to talk and ask questions showing a broad interest in your child above and beyond school?

Is there a homework policy? Ask: "Does the teacher require homework on a regular basis?" While some feel that homework in and of itself is not that important, it is important to know what the teacher's expectations are. Some teachers give no homework because they don't want to have to mark it. Ask: "When your child does work, do you and the child get a chance to see it after it has been corrected?" It is important that your child has work returned corrected and with comments. This is part of the learning process. To see whether this homework has been of any use, ask: "Do you have any papers that were returned so that I can see them?" You should look to see the types of comments made. Are they always negative, or are they balanced with positive comments? It is important to note which comments come first (e.g., positive and then negative). Are negative comments made in a destructive (sarcastic) manner? Does the teacher take interest not only in the grammatical correctness of the homework but also in the creativity of the content? Would the comments help your child improve his or her work?

• *What kind of person is the teacher?* This is a very important question to ask. Be as specific as you can. What does your child have to say about the teacher? Specifically, what does your child like and dislike about the teacher?

• *Does the teacher like children?* Although this question may seem ludicrous, it isn't. Teaching is a job, and some teachers don't have an inherent feeling or liking for children.

• *Is the teacher only work-conscious?* Does the teacher place emphasis on the social-emotional growth of your child and take an interest in learning about this aspect of the child?

• *Is the teacher flexible?* Does the teacher take a flexible approach to learning or does everything have to be done in one specific way?

• *Is the teacher writing-oriented?* Does the teacher rely heavily on learning through written assignments or are discussion activities used for teaching?

• *Is the teacher interested in your child's life outside of school?*

• *Is the teacher test-happy?* Does it seem that your child takes a test every day or none at all?

• *How does the teacher handle discipline?* The ability to control a classroom is an art. The way of disciplining (or better yet, setting limits) shows the maturity of the teacher and the teacher's ability to create a learning environment that provides its own discipline. You want to know if corporal punishment (spanking) is used. A teacher who shouts and yells or pulls hair may not be the teacher for your child.

• *Does the teacher provide a great deal of structure in the classroom?* Knowing the needs of your child and how he or she learns best will make this question very important. If you are aware that your child performs best under clear supervision as opposed to working independently, a teacher who provides structure may be best.

• *Does the teacher look for volunteers to help out in the classroom? Do you feel that the volunteers are used effectively?* Many teachers have parents come in to help in the classroom. However, they use them in "wasted" ways (e.g., taking the children to the bathroom, letting them sit in the corner and watch, or if they attempt to help, saying that it's not necessary).

• *Does the teacher appear to favor one group of children over another?* Ask: "Did you feel that the teacher may have been interested in some kids more than others?" Teachers have been known to take greater interest in academically talented students and less interest in those who don't catch on as quickly. The reverse is also true. Some teachers feel that smart students don't need as much attention and consequently neglect them.

• *Can you tell me about any good or bad experiences you had with this teacher?* A simple story can tell a great deal about a teacher.

• *"When you spoke with your child's teacher, was the teacher willing to meet with you if necessary?"* It is important that the teacher be sensitive to the need for a parent-teacher conference and initiate such a meeting.

The Teacher in Action

There is no better way to know which teacher is best for your child than to visit the teacher in the classroom. It is only there that you will be able to get a feeling for the tone of the classroom. This is most important because it is within this atmosphere that learning (or failure to learn) occurs. A good teacher should create an atmosphere conducive to learning.

There are differences of opinion about the classroom visit. Some feel that it is best to go unannounced, not allowing the school and the teacher to put on their best "face." Otherwise, rather than seeing the real classroom-teacher tone, you would be seeing something prepared especially for you. Others feel that it is best to call the school, talk to the principal, and discuss your reasons for visiting. If you are new to the area and have moved during the summer, a visit to the classroom cannot be arranged. If you moved during the school year, a visit can be worked out for you. The same is true if you already live in the school district and are trying to determine which teacher is best for your child the following year. If, however, you wish to visit the teacher and classroom because you are not happy with the choice you have made, it should be stated to the principal that you wish to visit to better understand your child's schoolday.

School officials have been known to object to a visit to a classroom, claiming that it would be disruptive if all parents wanted to visit. You have a right to visit the classroom, however, as well as to see a classroom for the next year. Be prepared. If you are put off or denied, say to the principal, "I am sure that you have nothing to hide, so I'm confused as to why you won't allow me to visit." If the principal still puts you off, state, "I'm sure that the state, under education law . . . meant that parents should be better informed by visiting the school." You will need to know the law if your state has one by calling ahead to the education department.

This statement, with the appropriate educational law quoted, may be adequate, and the principal will arrange for your visit. Or the principal may put you off by stating that such a request must be in writing. If so, in your letter you should not only request a visit but express your confusion over having to go through such formal steps. A copy of this request must also be sent to the superintendent of schools. The superintendent may not be aware of the principal's individual policy about visitation, which may not be in accord with the school district's policy.

If the principal still denies your right to visit the classroom, notify him or her in writing that you will be writing the superintendent of schools that you have been denied access to a classroom to observe a teacher. A copy of such a letter must also be sent to the chairperson of your board of education. Further obstruction may require appropriate legal action.

The Classroom Visit

The time to visit a classroom is after the first five weeks of school. When you visit, you hope to see the teacher and the class when their daily routine is most typical. Avoid preholiday and end-of-year visits or you will not necessarily get an accurate view.

Dress casually when you visit the classroom. This is not the time to show off your best wardrobe. The teacher should include you in some of the learning experiences, and being dressed up may prevent you from getting into it.

Let the teacher know when you arrive that you are willing to help. You may learn a great deal working and talking to the students in the classroom. As you help, don't hesitate to ask the students: "Is it fun in this classroom?" "Do you always work so hard (if that appears to be the case)?" "What is your favorite time of the day?" The openness with which they express their feelings may be a clue to the classroom environment.

REMEMBER: You are there to observe first and to work second. Should you be visiting the classroom to observe your child's present teacher, let the child know ahead of time. Children do not like to be surprised.

What to Look For
The following are observations you will want to make when visiting the classroom:

1. The first thing you will observe won't be the classroom. Is the school clean? Are the halls excessively noisy? Are there monitors in the hallways to prevent disruption? Are there students in the hallways who appear as if they shouldn't be there? Are there students standing outside of the classrooms for disciplinary reasons? If you are accompanied by the principal, do the children greet him or her and seem happy to see him or her? Does the principal greet the children by their first names?

   That may seem like a lot to observe before you even get to the classroom, but it is important because the tone of the classroom is affected by the tone of the school.
2. When you enter the classroom, how are you greeted by the teacher—graciously or with annoyance? If the teacher is comfortable with visitors, he or she should behave with ease. The teacher should introduce you to the class, stating, "Mr. or Mrs. D. is visiting today to observe what we do in class."

   Students will turn and look. If they look too long and do not return to their work, it may tell you that few people visit the classroom. Remember, supervisors of teachers should visit the classroom periodically. This means the principal. Don't forget to let the teacher know that you would like to move about the classroom but will stay out of the way.

3. Appearance of the classroom. Is the room overly covered with work? A room whose walls are too crowded with work may be distracting. A room without work on the walls may indicate that the teacher fails to see a way in which to reinforce good work. Is the work exhibited as a reward or is it part of an exhibit on which the class worked as a group? Is there a reading area with comfortable chairs and rugs, or are the desks lined up traditionally?

4. What is the teacher's relationship with the students? The teacher's ability to relate to the students is very important. Does the teacher seem to have a personality clash with all the students, with some, or just with your child? Does the teacher appear to see them and treat them as individuals?

5. Rating the teacher. The following checklist will help.

☐ Teacher's appearance. The teacher should be dressed casually but not overly so. A teacher who is dressed too formally may unconsciously be communicating a message to the students to keep their distance.

☐ Is the teacher at ease or does he or she appear uptight? A teacher who appears nervous or ill at ease creates a tense tone in the classroom.

☐ Is the teacher flexible? If there is an apparent change in the routine of the class while you visit, (e.g., the child who was supposed to present a project today is out sick), can the teacher accomodate and make changes or does the teacher appear to become upset? The following is a checklist to help you rate how the teacher teaches:

☐ Does the teacher lecture more than ten percent of the time or 15 minutes straight? The rule of thumb is that a teacher should talk about ten percent of the time, while the students should be talking ninety percent of the time. This tells you that the students are actively participating in the learning process.

☐ Does the teacher get the students to listen to one another? This is very important, as it lets your child know that peers are listening to what he or she has to say and teaches the child to listen to others besides the teacher. The teacher may do this by saying: "Scott, what did Julie mean?" "Bart, can you tell me what Krissy just said?" This forces active listening and participation in the learning process.

☐ Does the teacher always answer a question, or does the teacher force the students to discover the answer? This is very important in teaching problem solving. The teacher may do this by saying: "Let's see if we can figure out the answers," or by asking another student, "Jill, what do you think about that answer?"

☐ Does the teacher provide an atmosphere in which children can ask questions? If your child is afraid of making a mistake, active participation in learning will not occur. Does the teacher listen to wrong answers rather than cut them off? Does the teacher accommodate and make changes, or does the teacher appear to become upset?

☐ The teacher's voice. Does the teacher's voice or tone appear anxious or overly stern? Does the teacher use sarcasm or call a child a name (e.g., "dummy") even as a joke? Both demonstrate poor teaching skills.

☐ How do the children interact with the teacher? Do the students appear to have good give and take with the teacher, or is there an overformality to their interaction?

REMEMBER: Don't be misled by the bubbly or always jovial teacher. A stern teacher may be more effective.

☐ Does the teacher stay seated? How much time does the teacher stay seated? Does the teacher move among the students and appear at ease doing so? This helps set a more relaxed tone to the classroom than always having the students come to the teacher's desk. Notice who sits where. Do the girls and boys sit separately, or are they integrated? Does it appear that some children sit closer to the teacher for disciplinary reasons?

☐ Does the teacher use physical contact (e.g., hand on the shoulder while talking)? Physical contact can be useful in letting a student know that the teacher is present and as a gesture of involvement.

6. How the teacher teaches your child. The saying is that a teacher who teaches provides only a one-way street for educating, while a student who learns does so on a two-way street. In the first case, the student is a passive participant in the educational process while in the later, he is active.

(Correcting a wrong answer is very important, and the learning process cannot occur if wrong answers are cut off immediately. Some teachers look only for the right answer and pick children who will provide them with it. Does the teacher choose children who don't have their hands up? And if the teacher picks a child who doesn't know the answer, does the teacher accept the child's response of "I don't know"? Good teaching allows youngsters to honestly say that they don't know an answer without necessarily feeling embarrassment.)

☐ Would the teacher give your child time to think if the child did not know an answer?

Often, it is necessary to give a youngster time to think and arrive at an answer. This tells a child that the teacher wants the child to actively participate and, in order to involve the child, will wait for the answer.

☐ Does the teacher allow for discussion that may not be directly related to the main topic but is still relevent?

This shows some flexibility in learning. Sometimes an important point can be learned even though it comes up in the context of another subject. A good teacher can incorporate that point into the lesson.

☐ Does the teacher always stick to the book or is learning achieved through planned activities?

A planned activity forces active participation and learning in a more exciting way than simply sticking with the material provided in the textbook.

☐ Is the week too routine? Learning should not be scheduled routinely.

☐ If your child is shy, does the teacher actively involve him or her in the learning process? Often the shy child, being less assertive, will be lost in the group. A good teacher can actively involve all children at appropriate times.

7. Does the teacher maintain control over the classroom? While discipline is not a subject to be taught in schools, working within the framework of limits set up by the teacher is an important lesson. Does the teacher carry through on demands? A teacher, like other adults in your child's life, needs to be consistent. It is important that your child recognize the ground rules of the classroom and be held accountable when failing to follow them.
8. Does the teacher have a sense of humor? Humor is very important in setting the tone of the classroom. It eases the anxiety of failure and can provide a release for tension. Having fun at appropriate times is part of learning and living with a group.
9. Does the teacher appear to organize classroom time? When your child finishes assigned work in class, is the remaining time structured in such a way that additional work or activities can be done, or does the child wander around? Basically, does your child go from one work activity to another without being told?
10. Does the teacher appear to respect the children? The following is a checklist to determine the teacher's attitude toward your child. If some are answered in the negative, you may have a real problem.

☐ Is your child able to express an opinion?
☐ Does your child's opinion appear to be respected?
☐ Is the teacher energetic and enthusiastic?
☐ Is the teacher able to participate in the learning process with your child, or does the teacher maintain the teacher-student distance?
☐ Does the teacher appear to respect your child as a human being and individual or lump your child as just another student?
☐ Is the teacher interested only in your child's academic ability or interested in knowing "all of your child"?

You have now evaluated the school, seen the classroom, and observed the teacher. Although there is no guarantee that you will make the perfect choice, you will at least make a conscious and educated one. The importance of matching up your child with the proper classroom tone and the right teacher can never be under-estimated. These basic rules are applicable to elementary, middle (junior high school), and high school levels. Obviously, as your child gets older, you should be able to obtain more feedback directly from the child's appraisal of a teacher. *Your continued active partici-pation, even when your child is in high school, is still most im-portant. It tells your child that you care a great deal about and maintain an interest in his or her education.*

How to Request a Specific Teacher
While high school-level education may not allow you as much free-dom to pick a teacher for your child, the middle school and especially the elementary school levels do. Some schools have policies that preclude parents requesting certain teachers. This should not stop you. When asking, make direct statements, supported by facts that you have collected, about how your child's needs can best be met by the teacher of your choice. If the principal refuses, put your request in writing, stating your preference for a particular teacher(s). The letter should state that you feel that Mr. or Mrs. R. would best match up with your child's learning needs. List the reasons why you believe your choice is correct.

REMEMBER: Make a copy to be sent to the superintendent of schools.

When Things Are Going Wrong
It is very important that you be aware as soon as possible when your child and the teacher are at odds with each other or when the child is not actively involved in the learning process. The following is a list of danger signals that should indicate to you that you need to find out more:

• *"I'm not learning."* Often, you may not take your child seriously when he or she claims not to be learning. It may be an indication that the child is bored or the first signs of a conflict between the child and teachers or classmates.
• *"Teacher doesn't like me."* Your child may feel that the teacher doesn't like him. This creates an obstacle by becoming the primary focus for your child rather than learning.

• *Doesn't talk about the teacher.* Most children have many stories to tell about school, and it's important that parents listen to them. If your child stops talking about the teacher, there could be a problem..

• *Doesn't talk about the class.* Your child may be having a difficult time fitting into the class or fitting in with peers. If your child is unhappy, does not talk about class, or suddenly ceases to talk about class, it may be an early danger signal.

• *Psychosomatic complaints.* The sudden development of stomachaches or headaches before going to school may be a sign of an inner anxiety about the school or the teacher. It is important that you recognize the possible cause of the complaint and check with the teacher. This is also true if your child is spending time in the school nurse's office.

• *Never has homework.* The importance of carrying on the learning process outside of school provides some relevance for homework. If your child never has homework, there is usually a clear reason, and you should know about it.

• *Avoids homework.* If your child becomes upset over doing homework and seems to always want to get away from it, this may be related to frustration over the work itself and anxiety in school.

• *Time to play after school.* Your child needs time to unwind after school. Don't be fooled into thinking everything is all right if your child comes home and immediately sits down to study.

• *Proud of work.* Your child should be bringing work home that is both good and bad. If your child doesn't bring work home that he or she is proud of, it may be more than just a sign of poor school performance.

• *Assignments returned.* Your child should receive homework assignments corrected by the teacher. If the child says that the teacher doesn't return the work, you'd better find out what's happening. If work is returned without comments, contact the teacher and find out why.

• *Appropriate interaction.* If your child tells you that the teacher has called him or another child names, find out what is going on. This is also true for situations in which the teacher purposely embarrassed a child. Neither is a good teaching technique.

• *I'm sorry.* In talking with your child, find out whether the teacher ever admits she's wrong and says she's sorry. A child who is wrongfully accused and not absolved may carry a long-standing grudge against a teacher, who may remain unaware of the conflict.

• *Corporal punishment.* If your child reports that the teacher used physical force, find out whether this is school policy and discuss the situation with the teacher. Make it clear that you find the use of physical force a poor substitute for controlling a class in a constructive manner.

• *"I feel stupid."* Your child relates that he or she feels stupid in class. This may indicate that the work is at too high a level or that for unknown reasons the child isn't able to grasp the work. In either case, contact the teacher.

Having determined that your child is having difficulty in school, you will want to assess the situation. It's important not to immediately see your child as the victim and take on the teacher and the school as a cause. If you have picked the right teacher in the first place and your child shows the above danger signals, you will know that the teacher wants to communicate with you and your child. The right teacher wants learning to be a positive experience. The right teacher wants you to get in contact as soon as possible.

Contacting the Teacher

The initial contact with the teacher can be a note in which you state what you see as the problem or identify the danger signals. (Keep a copy.) It is important to be specific. Point out any of the previously mentioned danger signals. Be supportive rather than accusatory. Request that the teacher call you, or if the teacher would like to set up a conference, indicate when you are available. *Your* desire is to have the teacher on your child's side. *Your* aim is to determine how you can be of help to the teacher or can be of help at home.

Suggest that the conference include your child. Some teachers find it inhibiting to have a child present at such a conference. Involving a child as an active participant makes the child responsible to work on a resolution of the conflict or the situation.

The right teacher will respond to your note within a day because that teacher will want to know what is going on. When the teacher calls, continue to be supportive. Tell the teacher what you are seeing at home (the danger signals). Anticipate a positive response by the teacher until you get something else. Some teachers may view this as: "Oh my God! I have a parent on my back. How can I get free?" After you have talked on the telephone, if you feel that you and the teacher have clarified the situation and some concrete plans were made, your note will have accomplished its purpose.

If you receive no response to your note, call the school directly and ask to speak to the teacher. Most likely, you will have to leave your number, and the teacher will return your call. If you still don't get a response, notify the principal, who will want to know. When you speak to the principal, tell him first about your note (say that you have a copy) and then about your unanswered phone call. The principal should say: "I'll look into this and get back to you." He should get back to you within a day. If not, call again to find out why you haven't heard from him. Express your dismay. If you feel that the principal is not addressing the problem in a professional manner, contact the superintendent of schools by phone and then with a follow-up letter (make copies).

After speaking with the teacher, you may hang up the phone feeling that everything wrong is your fault and nothing is wrong with the school. If all the teacher did was complain about your child, the class, and the school; avoided specifics; and made no concrete suggestions to rectify the situation, it's very possible that you didn't get your message across. It is important, however, that you now wait two to three weeks. There may be a change in the situation, reflected by the fact that the danger signals have disappeared. This may indicate that the teacher got your message and made changes in the classroom.

Always let your child know that you talked with the teacher. Identify the problems and the reasons for speaking with the teacher. A few days later you will want to ask the child, "Did your teacher talk to you?" This will indicate the ability of the child and the teacher to communicate with each other. This will also set the stage should you and the teacher decide that a conference is necessary.

If you do not see any changes, and communication between you and the teacher is strained, you will have to set up a conference among you, the teacher, and the principal. In talking with the principal, say the following: "I am having a difficult time communicating with Mr. or Mrs. R. We (your child's teacher and you) can't seem to work together. I have tried to work with my child at home but hope the school can help."

If a conference is set up, bring along your list of danger signals, your copy of the note to the teacher, and notes of your phone conversation (any specific decisions or plans that may have been reached). It's important to be concise in your observations and specific in your complaints.

If it turns out that your choice of a teacher was wrong, you may have to change teachers. Unfortunately, you have to weigh the pros and cons of such a change. Obviously, if the classroom is so destructive that there is no chance for a constructive interaction between your child and the teacher, a change may have to be forced upon the school. This may be a decision made by the principal alone or in accordance with the superintendent of schools. Your child should not have to undergo such a change if you have found the right teacher.

POINTS TO REMEMBER

• Know your child and how the child learns. More important than knowing an IQ score is knowing how your child best learns and the kind of classroom environment in which he or she does this best. You will learn a lot about your child before he ever gets to first grade by observing him and talking to preschool and kindergarten teachers. Be objective.

• The tone of the classroom and the teacher who creates that tone are more important factors in helping your child learn than the actual materials presented. Matching your child with the right teacher is very important.

• Involving yourself in the school allows you to get information about teachers and school policy through the grapevine. This may be the best channel of information that allows you to make the best decision for the child.

• Talking to other parents, particularly those who have had children in the school level you are interested in, is a very good way to find out about a specific teacher or the teacher you may request for your child. Be specific, using the questions outlined earlier.

• Watching the teacher in action is the best way of finding out whether your child and the new teacher will have a positive learning experience together.

• Don't hesitate to communicate with the teacher if there are danger signals that your child's learning experience is not working out. Don't hesitate to call the principal. Parents worry about retaliation against their children. This should never be the case. Should this happen, appropriate action can be taken.

REMEMBER: A positive educational experience can have a great deal of influence on the child's future. A negative experience must be met by you, the parent, whenever it occurs, and as soon as possible.

Lunchrooms

Lunchrooms in schools (otherwise known as the school cafeteria) can be most important places in the course of the school day. More often, they're not because school systems see them as necessary but inconvenient nuisances in the daily routine. Schools usually ignore the social and learning aspect of the time children spend in the lunchroom and see it as only a time to provide nutrition to the students. For those of you who still can remember eating with your teachers, that is something that has long since slipped into the past. Instead, from first grade to twelfth, lunches are highly supervised and regimented periods. Because of the regimentation, your child and his or her peers can view the lunch period as a time to act up. This has caused the removal of such foods as peas and peanuts from the menu in order to prevent any reoccurrence of food fights.

Schools generally have the philosophy that children should be fed quickly and efficiently. The basic idea is to get children in and out of the lunchroom as fast as possible. One senses among school staff the "time bomb" fear of the lunchroom period. Yet although the nonnutritional functions of the lunchroom have generally been ignored, the nutritional aspects have recently received a great deal of necessary attention. The natural food proponents as well as the anti-junk food groups have made school officials, cafeteria managers, and food directors take a more careful look at what goes into the lunchroom menu. But you must learn to look as well.

Lunchrooms tend to be utilitarian, generally reflecting a lack of interest by those who design them. One can only hope that some day one-tenth of the time taken to design a gymnasium will be taken to design a lunchroom. Although newer school buildings have included lunchrooms with more windows and brighter colors, they still are box-shaped rooms with corners. Lunchrooms could be round, with food being distributed in the center rather than from a side or corner. If you listen to your child, find out how long it takes to obtain food. If the lunch period is twenty-five minutes and it takes your child ten minutes or more to get food, think about the fact that the child has to eat in ten minutes (allowing for five minutes to unload the tray and go on to the next class). Some school officials will say that ten minutes is all children need to eat lunch. Remember that they do not see the social benefits of the lunch period. They ignore the socialization process that for some children is very important.

Lunchrooms in different school systems have various structures. This is true for elementary, middle, and high school. The elementary school-age child is the most heavily regimented. Children who bring lunch are often segregated from children who buy lunch (the hot lunch). Many times, your child may suddenly not wish to bring lunch to school. The reason may simply be that the child wants to sit with friends and can't because he or she brings lunch from home (the cold lunch) while the friends buy a hot lunch. Even if children are not discriminated against because of the lunch they eat, they still may not choose with whom they will eat lunch. As they come into the lunchroom, they are often herded to one table, and when that one is filled up, another table is started.

The primary aim of school officials is to have the children eat as quickly as they can so that they can be sent outside to play. That the lunchroom is considered a nonsocialization, all-business affair is also shown by the fact that some schools dim the lights in the cafeteria while children are eating, further reinforcing the idea that this is not a time to talk. At times, your child may wear a coat while eating. This cuts down the amount of time it takes to get everyone outside after lunch.

Not all schools are like this. The fact still remains that few schools take the nonnutritional aspects of the school lunchroom program seriously or see it as a learning experience.

To be informed, you must ask your child the following: "Whom do you sit with at lunchtime? Do your teachers tell you where to sit?" "How long does it take you to get your lunch, eat it, and clean up?" "What rules do you have to follow in the lunchroom?" "Is the lunchroom clean?"

You may be surprised that your child can answer every one of those questions. School officials seldom ask them because they don't believe the lunchroom is an important place in your child's life.

REMEMBER: When evaluating your child's lunchroom, you are looking at more than just where the child eats. You have a chance to better understand the school as a whole. And if you don't like the lunchroom, you may also find that you don't like the school.

The Basic Lunch

The best way to ensure that your child has a nutritious lunch is to make it for the child and send it to school. However, there are advantages to buying lunch in school: the variety, the convenience (making a lunch at seven in the morning 180 days a year can get to you), the fact that it is generally inexpensive, and the fact that it is hot. To begin to understand the lunch menu, you first need to find out in what way, if any, the school participates in federally funded programs. If the school is involved with federal programs, it is required to use the commodities provided by the government. Thus, the menu will revolve around these commodities. This may explain the heavy reliance on chicken or hamburger. (It may be the "protein of the month.") Guidelines for the nutritional content of a lunch are clear and follow the outline below:

TYPE "A" LUNCH
2 oz. lean meat or fish
1 slice enriched bread
½ pint fluid milk
¾ cup of vegetable
¾ cup of fruit
1 tsp. enriched margarine or butter

The above represents a lunch pattern that is government-approved. It is the basis of most school lunch programs but can be altered by some school boards, for example, as in New York State. The changes can be made in what is "offered" (all five components are available to be picked from) versus "served" (all five components are automatically served regardless of whether the children want them). In the latter case, the amount of "plate waste" is tremendous, since there is no one in the lunchroom who is going to stand over the children and make sure they eat everything on the plate.

To find out more about what is served in school, you need to look at the menu. This should be sent home to you monthly or may be printed in your local newspaper. In either case, it is a *must* that you receive some notification about what will be served. The menu will reflect the following:

• *Favorite foods:* Various parts of the country serve foods that are more indigenous to the people in their communities. The southwestern part of the United States is more apt to serve tacos than the northeastern part. Pasta meals (using spaghetti or macaroni) are probably more heavily relied on by schools in New York. Furthermore, lunchroom personnel have discovered that children generally don't like to try anything new, and so the menu reflects the "old reliables."

• *Circle menus:* Looking over the menu, you will see that there is a predictable pattern. Both you and your child have come to look for hamburgers on Monday, fish sticks on Wednesday, and spaghetti on Thursday. But in between, there should be variety and a chance to try some new lunches.

• *Seasonal changes:* The menu should reflect changes in the seasonal availability of foods, such as more fruits in the spring and early fall.

What the menu won't show you is the other foods being served, mainly junk food. This is a part of the lunch program after the elementary school years; for some school districts, it is primarily a money-making proposition, as there is a high profit in these items. There is no reason for any lunch program to provide bags of potato chips or cans of soda. These can be replaced easily by fresh fruit juices, cheese and crackers, vegetable packages, and organic foods.

To fully understand the lunch program, you will have to visit the cafeteria. You may want to involve other parents; should you discover things you wish to change, you will need their support. To visit the lunch program, you will probably have to call and make arrangements with the principal and the lunchroom manager. *There should be no reason why you cannot visit.* Express your interest in knowing what the children eat, where they eat it, and the manner in which it is served.

Once in the lunchroom, look for the following:

- The time it takes for the children to obtain lunch, eat lunch, and deposit (unload) the lunch trays.
- The manner in which children find a place to sit. Are they told where to sit or can they choose their own places?
- If you are observing an elementary school, remember, the school's object is efficiency, or getting the children in and out quickly.
- If you are visiting a middle or high school, participation is the concern of lunchroom personnel. See how many students actually eat. The money you gave for lunch may not be used for lunches. Remember, dieting can be the "in" thing in high school.
- Go through the lunch line and see the size of the portions. The amount obviously changes from elementary school to high school, but sometimes the portions are not enough.
- See the types of foods offered that are not on the menu. Is there a lot of junk food or none at all? Would you like to eat lunch there? Are there foods that appeal to you?
- Is there a provision for children who need a special diet (e.g., diabetic children)? Some school districts have no provision for special lunches, and some states have no law that forces them to provide special lunches.

You should be concerned if:

- It takes more than five minutes for children to be served, leaving less than twelve to fifteen minutes to eat lunch.
- There is seating discrimination because some children bring lunch and others buy theirs, or vice versa.
- The selection process is sharply limited, with junk food being sold and bought, and there are few available fresh foods. There is no selection in the elementary schools because school personnel do not believe that children that age can make a choice.

• Your child is still hungry and, in fact, comes home not just for a snack but to consume a meal. The portions may be inadequate.
• Your child is hurried out of the lunchroom by direct intervention ("It's time to go") when he or she is only half done, or the child wears a coat in order to save time in going outside to the playground.

If you are unhappy with what you see, make notes, because you will need them to compile a list of complaints. These should be presented directly to the district lunch managers. The lunch manager may be sympathetic, but school district policy may set down the guidelines. The manager may be interested in your help to change some of the lunchroom policies.

If the school lunch manager is unsympathetic to your concerns and appears to have a negative reaction, you will have to contact the state school lunch personnel officer. You need to find out why the menu is set up the way it is. Calling this person has two advantages: You may gain information the school lunch manager would not offer, and you can state your concerns to state officials who can look into the matter.

REMEMBER: Follow up with a letter to the state school lunch personnel.

Suggestions for a Better Lunch Program

The following list contains suggestions you can make in trying to improve the lunch program.

• More time to eat.
• Seeing the lunch program as a chance for learning. For example, puppet shows can be set up during lunchtime in the elementary school, a worthwhile project for the school's PTA.
• "Let's get rid of junk food." A contest could be held among the students to find alternatives to junk food.
• Selection of foods for the elementary schoolchild.
• A youth advisory council set up to advise the school lunch manager at the middle and high school levels (or at least feedback on a regular basis at all levels from those who have to eat the school lunch).

Students' Records

The Family Educational Rights and Privacy Act of 1974 that gave parents the right to inspect and possibly change children's school records was probably one of the strongest pieces of legislation passed by the federal government to protect children's individual rights. In passing the act, Congress recognized the need of parents to have access to their children's educational records. In so doing, Congress notified school districts that received money from the United States Office of Education (which includes practically all school districts to varying degrees) that they had to abide by a set of rules giving new powers to parents or lose funding. Despite the importance of this legislation, few school officials are fully aware of the law's requirements. Teachers, as well, are not always informed that most of the written comments they make about children are now available to parents.

The importance of the act cannot be minimized. It provides a legal guarantee for children's educational rights. In order to implement the law, it is first necessary to understand it.

The act gives certain rights to parents regarding their children's educational record. Your child gains the same rights that you have once he or she reaches the age of eighteen or is attending any school beyond the high school level (thus becoming an eligible student). The following are the rights given by the act:

• A school must allow parents or eligible students to inspect and review the students' education records maintained by the school. This includes any information in handwriting, print, tapes, and film kept by the district. The only exception would be a personal record kept by the school staff that was made as a personal memory aid and is in the personal possession of the individual who made it; such information cannot be revealed to any other person except a substitute staff member.

• Parents and eligible students may request that a school correct records believed to be inaccurate or misleading. If the school refuses to change the records, you have a right to request a formal hearing (to be discussed later in this section).

• Generally, the school must have written permission from the parent or eligible student before releasing any information from a student's record.

While this information provides a general understanding of the act's intent concerning rights of access to children's educational records, the act goes on to define policy guidelines for the school districts that maintain those records. They are required annually to notify you of the following policies concerning the education record:

• The right to inspect and review educational records.
• Guidelines to limit the disclosure of information in the education records (who can and cannot see the information).
• How to go about correcting information believed to be inaccurate, misleading, or in violation of the child's rights.
• The right for you to file a complaint with the department of education if the school district violates the act.
• The location of the child's educational records along with the types of records, names, and titles of school officials responsible for those records.
• Any practices that the school district wishes to employ concerning those records—for example, if it is the policy of the school district that a school official must be present when you are inspecting the records.

Along with these policies, the act further requires that the school district have written guidelines on disclosure of records to other school officials (teachers included) as long as they have "legitimate educational interests." For instance, does a teacher not directly involved in teaching your child have the right to look at the child's record? If "directory-type" information (e.g., name, address, telephone number, date and place of birth, honors and awards, activities, health status, and parents' marital status) is to be disclosed without permission, the school district must tell you the type of information that is classified in this manner. They must also provide you with a reasonable amount of time to tell the school not to reveal directory information about your child. The school district will acknowledge that it will maintain an accurate record of all requests for information and of who was granted access to the child's educational records.

Having reviewed the basic intent of the act, it is important to remember that the school district may not be familiar with the requirements or give as much public display as the law intended. For you and your child, the important thing is to have access to the records and the ability to change those parts of the record (if any) that are inaccurate.

REMEMBER: The school district does not have to consider a request to change the grade your child received from a teacher.

Gaining Access

Gaining access requires that you contact the school and find out what procedure you need to follow. If you are informed that the school district will not allow you access, you will have to make a formal request and obtain a written refusal. Whether you receive a written refusal or not, you will next need to contact

Family Educational Rights and Privacy Act Office
Room 526 F
Humphrey Building
200 Independence Avenue, S.W.
Washington, D.C. 20201
Telephone: (202) 245-7488

If you have been informed by the school district that you can inspect the educational record, it is important that you (this also may be a policy of the school district) put that request in writing. On the following page is a sample request letter (make a copy).

If the letter sounds formal, it is meant to be. By quoting the law under which you make your request, you notify school officials that they are required to act within guidelines that are clearly defined. Furthermore, should the school official you initially spoke with agree to your request but then have the decision reversed by a superior, the letter will save you a wasted trip.

Name
Address
City, State, Zip Code
Date

Records Access Officer
Name of School District
Address of School District
City, State, Zip Code

Re: Family Educational Rights and Privacy Act Request

Dear Records Access Officer:

Under the provisions of the Family Educational Rights and Privacy Act, I request access to inspect my son or daughter's (name of child) cumulative record.

Should there be any fee involved for copying the record or parts of it, please let me know ahead of time.

If for any reason you deny my request, please inform me of the reasons for the denial in writing and provide the name and address of the person or body to whom an appeal should be directed. I would appreciate hearing from you as soon as possible. Thank you for your consideration.

Sincerely,

Signature

How to Change the Educational Record

Having gained access to your child's educational record, you may want to have the principal or other school official explain any questions you have about the record. Let them be helpful. You actually may learn more than is in the written record. If you find inaccuracies, misleading statements, or information that you feel violates the child's rights, discuss it with the principal. There may be errors that the principal will see the need to change. If you feel you need to correct any other information, you have the right to try to amend the record. The school district is required to have a minimum policy under which to proceed. The procedure should be as follows:

1. You should identify the part of the record you want changed and specify why you feel that the information is inaccurate, misleading, or in violation of the child's rights. You then need to ask the school district to amend the record. (This must be done in writing.)
2. The school district may comply with the request or decide not to comply. If it decides not to comply, it must notify you of the decision and advise you of your right to a hearing to challenge the information believed to be inaccurate, misleading, or in violation of the child's rights.
3. You must then advise the school district if you want to challenge the record in a hearing.
4. The school district must notify you, reasonably in advance, of the date, place, and time of the hearing.
5. The hearing must be conducted by an officer who is a disinterested party, but the hearing officer can be an official of the school district. It is required of the school district that they provide you with a full and fair opportunity to present evidence relevant to the issues raised in the original request (see part 1 of this list) to amend the educational record. You may want help. Contact a lawyer.
6. The school district must prepare a written decision based solely on the evidence presented at the hearing. The written decision must include a summary of the evidence presented and the reasons for the decision.
7. If the school district decides, based on evidence presented, not to amend the record, you have a right to place in the record a statement commenting on the challenged information or a statement setting forth reasons for disagreeing with the decision.
8. If the school district decides that the information included was inaccurate, misleading, or in violation of the child's rights, the record must be appropriately amended, and you must get notification to that effect.

If your request is denied, before accepting it as fact, call or write the Family Educational Rights and Privacy Act Office.

The cumulative educational record is the ongoing reporting system that the school district maintains on your child. Given its importance, others (Congress) felt that it was equally important that you have the right to monitor it and to know what it does and does not contain. States such as New York have record retention and disposition schedules, which automatically delete material from educational records. It is important that you know something about your state's regulations.

If nothing more, the Family Educational Rights and Privacy Act of 1974 gives you the ability to ensure that your child's educational rights are not violated.

Reading a Report Card

Report cards are used by the school to let you know how your child is performing in the classroom. It is the reporting system used by most school systems. There have been changes in the type of reporting done since you went to school. For the most part, however, it is similar to the way in which you were probably graded. Unfortunately, the reporting systems used today are not sophisticated enough for the transfer of sufficient information from the teacher to you. That means that the information the teacher wants to communicate to you cannot be completely transmitted by way of the report card.

Report cards tend to be divided into two categories: the educational development of the child, and the child's social-behavioral development. At the elementary school level, there is usually a place in the report card for a comment giving the teacher an opportunity to share with you his or her general feelings about your child. At the secondary school level (middle and high school), this is not always the case. Thus, you are looking at a very unsophisticated reporting system that you will *only partially* rely on to understand how your child is functioning in school. It is important to remember that the report card is the formal way to communicate and becomes a part of the official record. To put report cards in perspective, remember that the use of the informal methods of keeping track of your child's school progress is through your ongoing involvement in the school program and with the teacher.

Report cards are one-dimensional reporting systems. Because they are part of the educational process, it is important to learn how to understand them, read between the lines, and recognize danger signals communicated by the reporting system.

If you are like most parents, you will first look at the grades (letter grades or percentages). Unfortunately, while a C grade reflects "average" work, the reporting system used by most schools tends to make that grade seem below average. This results from the fact that an A grade should reflect superior work and a B grade above-average work. Psychologically, the placement of the C grade third down the list makes it appear to be below average. Furthermore, many families have difficulty accepting average work in their child, equating "average" with being slow.

The first step in looking at the report card is to determine the level of work being performed in the class. For instance, the report card should be able to tell you the range of reading levels in the class. The reading levels of the children in a fourth grade class may range from a level expected of a child in the beginning of the fifth grade down to a level expected of a child at the end of the third grade. Thus, if your child is obtaining an A grade in reading but is reading material expected of someone still in the third grade, the child is functioning below a level expected of someone his or her age. *You must find out the range of achievement in the class in order to fully understand the significance of your child's grades.* You will also want to know how many children in the class are reading at the various levels so that you can determine where your child is functioning within the class. Most reporting systems not only provide a grade but attempt to tell you whether the child is working below or above ability, in other words, what kind of effort the child is putting into schoolwork. Thus, if your child receives a B grade with a *poor* effort, the teachers are telling you that your child could do better. A B grade with a *good*-effort comment says that your child is working at a level the teacher feels is appropriate. A typical report card may have the following effort scale in association with a grade:

A - Superior
B - Good
C - Average
D - Below average
F - Failing

Parent conferences are very important additions to all reporting systems. If the school does not set up a parent conference at the time of the first report card (for that school year), call to set one up. If the school tries to dissuade you, clearly state your purpose: "I wish to set up a conference with my child's teacher so that I can clear up some confusion on the report card."

REMEMBER: The right teacher for your child will want to meet with you.

Requesting the conference should let the teacher know that you are interested in the child's education and performance in the classroom and that the reporting system used is inadequate by itself in telling you how the child performs both educationally and socially in the classroom.

The Report Card

Often, you can find inconsistencies in the report card, which should raise questions. Most of the danger signals, as we will identify them, probably represent inconsistencies. It will be these inconsistencies which you will want to follow up. The common danger signals you will need to be aware of include the following:

• An inconsistency between the marks the child obtains and the comments given by the teacher. At times the child may receive a poor grade with the accompanying remarks that the child "tries hard" or "is attentive in class." It is important to find out what is preventing the child from achieving a better grade, given the child's ability to apply himself. Another common inconsistency is seen when your child obtains a high grade but the comments state that she is "sloppy in her work" or "doesn't pay attention." Again, it is important to find out why there is a difference between the grade and the comment.

• Learning comments are inconsistent with social comments. If your child is receiving poor grades in class but receives social comments such as "He's a joy to have in class," you will want to find out why. Is your child so nice that the teacher is willing to accept lower-quality work?

• Inconsistencies between grades received in math in comparison to reading. A general rule to follow is that a "good" student is good in all major subjects. It is unusual for a child to be an A student in math and a C student in reading. You will want to find out why. Does you child have a specific learning problem?

• There should be no surprises on a report card. Again, it is important to remember that the report card is the formal and official way for the teacher to tell you about your child's performance in the classroom. If you have maintained contact with the teacher so that communication between you continues throughout the year, and if you have been talking frequently with your child about the school day, there should be no surprise grades or comments on the report card.

The Straight-A Report Card

While it can be very comforting for your child to receive all A grades on the report card, it should raise the question of whether the educational program is challenging enough. The question you will want to ask is, "At what level is my child being instructed?" A bright child receiving A grades at a level of work below what he or she can do may not be profiting educationally.

If the report card shows marked differences in grades (from A grades to C grades), you will want to know why. Does it show that your child and the teacher are not able to cooperate in learning as well as they did the year before? Is there something occurring emotionally within your child that is interfering with the ability to learn during this reporting period as opposed to the previous period? All are reasonable questions that you should answer yourself. For instance, are there problems at home?

You should remember the following points:

• Report cards are informational in purpose; that is, they are the formal and official way to let you know how your child is performing in school.

• Comments on report cards tend to be nonspecific, probably because teachers know that a report card is shared with the child. Thus, private perceptions of your child that the teacher may want to share with you will not be found in the comment part of the report card.

• Your child, even if bright and receiving good grades, needs a parent conference. This should occur at least once a year, regardless of the educational level (kindergarten through twelfth grade) of your child. This shows your child that you are interested in the educational program. This demonstrates to the teacher that you are interested in more than grades.

A Comment About Parent-Teacher Conferences
Report cards not only tell you about the child's performance in the classroom but provide further information about the teacher. If you have found the right teacher for your child, then he or she will want to participate in a conference with you. Conferences provide you the opportunity to ask about the following:

• How your child is doing socially and emotionally in the classroom. Are there differences between how the child handles himself at home and in the classroom? You may be surprised that your child acts very differently in one setting as opposed to the other.
• It should help you understand the relationship between your child and his or her teacher.
• It provides you with the opportunity to find out what the norm or range of performances is in the child's classroom. Don't be afraid to ask for representative scores among the child's classmates.
• It should help you determine more accurately whether the teacher feels that your child is achieving at the expected level.
• It provides both you and the teacher an informal and private opportunity to discuss areas of concern that cannot be transmitted because of the limitations of the report card.

Educational Regulations
The school district is required by state law to follow certain regulations in order to provide your child with an education. These regulations were designed to provide guidelines within which children can obtain a public education (private schools do not have to adhere to the regulations as strictly) as well as to provide some uniformity within a given state.* The regulations that govern primary education can vary from those governing secondary education.

---

*Private schools, in order to receive accreditation, must meet certain requirements. However, they still are less restricted by state regulations than public schools.

The differences from state to state are even greater. Should you move from one state to another, the regulations governing the school district can vary greatly. What remains constant throughout the United States is not the specifics of the regulations but rather the general intent and the areas to which they apply.

Knowledge of state education laws and regulations can be very helpful. It is unrealistic to expect to be an expert in the law or to retain for instant recall all of the numerous facts. You do have to be familiar with the general areas of education that are governed by regulations and know that there are state agencies whose purpose is to ensure that the school district is adhering to the law. Understanding state legal standards that govern educational policy within the school district is absolutely necessary when and if you need to advocate for your child. Although this sounds complicated and legalistic, it isn't. If you are willing to follow some basic guidelines and make a few telephone calls or write a letter or two, you will have done all that is initially required. Although it may be easier to wait until there is a crisis, it is better to be partially prepared ahead of time.

All state education departments maintain legal staffs. At the time your child enters school, you should write or call (although more expensive, a call gives you an opportunity to state your purpose more clearly) the legal department of the state education department. By doing this, you have already taken a big step. Knowing the telephone number, address, or an individual official's name makes the remaining process, if and when you need it, move more quickly and can even give you a sense of familiarity.

In contacting the state education department, your goal is to obtain general information about the laws that regulate and set legal standards for the provision of education. At this time, you may wish to learn what appeals mechanisms your state education department provides should you feel that the school district is not adhering to a regulation. Furthermore, you may discover that the state education department maintains a hot line to handle complaints and crises as they occur.

State education laws and regulations are numerous and at times complex. The following represent general areas that are governed by these regulations and some that you should be aware of for future references.

• *Admission requirements.* Admission requirements are defined clearly by all states. Most states require that children reach the age of five before they can be admitted to kindergarten and the age of six before entering the first grade. The date for attaining the required age varies from state to state. Furthermore, most states require as a prerequisite for admission that children undergo a medical examination as well as being immunized against contagious diseases.

• *Attendance requirements.* Most states require children to attend school once they have attained a certain age and to remain in school until they have reached another specific age. All states have guidelines for exemption from compulsory attendance. In some states, there are as many as a dozen reasons for exemption.

• *Attendance enforcement agent.* Almost all states have regulations that govern the enforcement of attendance requirements. The responsibility is usually left to the school district. State codes detail the process to which the attendance officer must adhere in enforcing the laws. Finally, the regulations of each state clearly define the consequences for children who fail to attend school.

• *Curriculum.* In all states, the curriculum offered by the school districts is prescribed by the state. The degree of control exercised over the school district varies from state to state. Guidelines regulating the number, quality, and content of the courses that the school district provides are controlled by the state. In most states, failure to meet these curriculum guidelines can affect accreditation of a school.

• *Extracurricular activities.* The school district is for the most part mandated to provide a wide range of nonacademic activities, such as school organizations (usually not including secret societies) and athletic competition. Some states require that these activities occur at both the primary and secondary school levels. Most states provide a general statement encouraging school districts to ensure broad student participation by providing a balanced program.

• *Guidance and counseling program.* Almost all states provide guidelines for the establishment of guidance and counseling programs for school districts. Guidance programs are usually defined as services designed to diagnose and support your children as they obtain an education. Some states define the types of services that your district *must* provide.

- *High school graduation requirements.* All states have clear provisions that must be met for graduation from high school. These requirements may be met through the acquisition of credits but also, in some states, require the passing of a standardized test.
- *Individual pupil records.* All states have regulations that govern the maintenance of pupil records. These regulations govern a number of areas including content, who shall keep the records, who shall have access to them, and rules determining retention and disposition.
- *Promotion requirements.* It is interesting to note that few states have provisions that deal with promotion requirements.
- *Pupil-teacher ratio.* Most states regulate the number of students in a class, otherwise called the pupil-teacher ratio. This changes from the primary to the secondary school level. There are usually guidelines for calculating the pupil-teacher ratio.
- *School calendar.* All states have requirements for the minimum number of days school must be in session during a calendar year. Furthermore, there are provisions specifying the length of the school day.
- *Textbook requirements.* While the school district has the power to adopt textbooks for use in the educational program, this power is limited by state regulations. Many states require that textbooks be selected from a list provided by the state. Some local school districts can select any textbook they desire.

When considering state regulations that govern the school district, it is also important to remember that some of the requirements are affected by teacher contracts and are part of the general collective bargaining process.

When questioning a state regulation, you first go to the principal and express your concerns. Should you feel that you have not received a satisfactory answer, you can proceed to the board of education. It is important to remember that if you feel that you are not receiving full information, you just might not be getting it. School officials, for the most part, become very anxious when a parent begins to discuss state regulations that govern education. School attorneys, because they are hired by the school district, are not always helpful. As we have already discussed, your final source for information is the state education department.

What has just been outlined is the "up the ladder" philosophy of gathering information. Simply stated, you go to the next higher source of information until you feel satisfied by the answers, although it is important to remember that the answers may not be the ones you wish to hear. At each step along the way, you can employ the following statements to obtain additional information: "Who else can tell me what I need to know?" "Why don't I give you a day or two and call back."

An important source of information is the National Institute of Education, Washington, DC 20208. As part of the Department of Education, it is their responsibility to gather information concerning educational policy that affects education.

Knowing how to gather information is at times more important than the information itself. Educational systems, like most other systems, allow you to assert your rights in order to ensure that your child receives an adequate education, but it is a rare educational system that will initiate that activity itself.

Testing

Educational testing has become as much a part of modern education as reading, writing, and arithmetic. We live in a society that relies too heavily on tests in order to determine what children know and should be able to learn. Rather than relying on those who know your child best—the child's teachers—educational systems turn to testing to supply the answers. Testing has been challenged because it fails to consider cultural differences, emotional state (mood) at the time of testing, and ability to perform under test conditions. Unfortunately, lasting judgments may be made on the basis of a single test. Along with these drawbacks to testing, there is another that is seldom discussed. The language used to describe the results on any given test may be more sophisticated than the measurements used to determine those results. This leads to a description of the child that is technically more advanced than the degree of sophistication of the test.

By labeling your child, the educational system can then place him or her in the "appropriate" learning niche. This is the lumping method of education. The assumption here is that children of a certain chronological age are ready to learn certain information. The advantage of this method is that it is economical. "Economical" becomes synonymous with "efficient." This system totally ignores the possibility that your child may not be "educationally programmed" in the same way as another child. Given the same amount of time, your child could learn the required information. The difference, which isn't taken into account, is that your child may need to learn or assimilate information in an order different from that of his classmates. For example, your child becomes interested and *motivated* to learn multiplication before learning subtraction. Since your child has the desire to learn the material "out of order" (the usual order being subtraction before multiplication), a program could be designed that would capitalize on this motivation rather than forcing your child to learn these math functions in the "typical" order.

Educational testing universally applied can serve many purposes. It can be a preschool screening device to determine the readiness of a child for the educational process. It can be used to determine the level of achievement, given a youngster's age in comparison to other children. It can clarify the important difference between "chronological immaturity" (delayed development) and a "permanent delay." Chronological immaturity can be defined as having the innate ability (the intellectual tools) to achieve but because of a general immaturity not achieving at a certain level (sometimes referred to as "not living up to potential"). "Permanent delay" is defined by the fact that the child simply does not have the innate ability to achieve and thus *will always* underachieve when compared with peers. In the first case, time is the theoretical remediator. In the second, overachievement would be necessary.

Testing can be used to determine why a child is not learning. Unfortunately, there are times when the answers provided do not lead to a remedial program but provide the education system with an excuse. Educational testing can be viewed in two very different ways. The first is to consider it as a screening device. Screen testing is testing applied to a group of children (e.g., the same class level) at the same time. The second type of educational testing, diagnostic testing, is intended to describe in depth a "problem area" related to a child's learning ability. Diagnostic testing, unlike screen testing, is given not to a group of children but to only one child at a time.

Rather than looking for a level at which the child is achieving, its purpose is to explain why the child is not achieving at the expected level and to describe possible remedial steps.

It is most important that you know what tests will be used (screening, diagnostic), when they will be given to your child, and for what purpose.

Screening Tests

The first screening test your child will face is the preschool screening. At the time of registration, specifically ask: "Will my child be taking any educational tests?" If so, ask: "What tests will be given and for what purposes?"

These two questions may be the most important ones you ask the school system. Finding out the evaluative procedure of the school may give you the best clues about the school's educational philosophy.

There are certain rules to remember about testing:

• Screening tests (testing applied to a group of children of the same age level) should not measure the progress of the individual child but rather the progress of the group of children tested within the system. When your child takes a screening test, it should not measure individual performance, rather, the testing should measure how the system in which the child is learning has progressed. It should answer the question, Have the fourth grade classes in your child's school system progressed from level A to level B (a higher level of achievement) as a result of the educational program applied by the school system, or has the achievement been only partially successful?

• Screen testing pits your child against the system. Unfortunately, few educational systems take the position about screen testing described above. Thus, it is your child versus the system. How well does the child perform compared with peers?

• Educational testing is not as sophisticated as we may think. While it can be a useful instrument, as part of the defining process it does not have the authority we attribute to it. School systems have a tendency to overrely on testing.

• Screen testing can be used in two very different ways. It can be used to screen out (the exclusive approach) or to define need, and it has no relevance to admittance (the inclusive approach). The exclusive approach would use testing to segregate a child into another program (e.g., a special class). The inclusive approach would attempt to accommodate the child in the already existing program (e.g., mainsteaming). In the former, screen testing is used to identify the *differences* in your child and use them to find another placement. The latter system attempts to find the similarities between your child and others of the same age in order to maintain the child with his or her present group.

Find out what screening tests will be given to your child. Remember, the school has to have your permission to administer any tests. Once the screening tests are given, you may or may not hear from the teacher. The teacher (often the guidance counselor in the middle school or the high school) is the person who gets the results of the screening tests. These test results may not automatically be shared with you. If you don't hear about them, you have a right to request to see the results. If the school feels that they have identified a problem, you should be notified. It is important to remember that if the school carries out a screening test that identified a problem in your child's ability to learn, interventions must be provided.

Preschool screening tests should look at various skills to determine how mature the child is and provide a general sense of whether the child is ready to enter kindergarten. The areas looked at include the following:

• *Motor skills.* A review of motor skills to determine gross motor (general coordination ability) and fine motor (using the hands in more refined activities such as scissoring, etc.) ability.

• *Speech development.* A general assessment of communication skills, use of words and sentences, and speech dysfluencies such as hesitancy or stuttering.

• *Letter, color, and number recognition skills.* This provides basic information about what the child already knows before entering school.

• *Vision and hearing.* This is intended to ensure that the child has no disabilities in areas that would interfere with the ability to learn.

• *Maturation level.* A cursory assessment of the child's ability to use a classroom situation and the child's emotional functioning.

Screen testing is usually given yearly and is referred to as "achievement" testing. Again, the school system will use these tests to determine how your child compares with other children at the same age level. These tests are standardized, and many are used nationally. Some states, such as New York, have devised additional tests given at predetermined grade levels (e.g., third, sixth, etc.) in order to determine the child's level of achievement and use them to determine whether the child should be promoted. This type of testing will describe the math and reading level of a child and compare it with other students at the same level. Many times, it will also provide a score that can be translated into an intelligence quotient (IQ).

Finding Out the Results

The process of obtaining the results of screening tests will usually be initiated by the school through a parent-teacher conference. If this doesn't occur, call the teacher. There may be a valid reason for any delay. If no time has been set aside to go over the tests with you, request time. You *must find out how the information on the screening test is going to be used. It may explain otherwise confusing decisions the school makes about your child.*

Make sure that you bring a pad of paper and a pencil to the conference. The language used to describe your child's performance on these tests can be confusing, and writing down the information is very useful. If you can keep in mind the following points, you will find it easier to understand the results.

• Always ask that test results be discussed in terms of percentages. Unless you are used to dealing with statistics, you will find the other forms of reporting confusing. If the school staff starts giving the test results in "standard deviations" or "stanine" (both are statistical ways of comparing a child's performance with the average performance), ask them: "Please explain these scores in terms of percentages for me." Percentages make it easier for you because you can visualize 100 children, with so many performing ahead of your child and so many behind.

• Always ask for local norms as opposed to national norms. Test reporting can be done in terms of how a child does against the normal values of children in the United States. Local norms compare the child's performance against children within his or her sociocultural background (e.g., school district or state). National norms tend to make the child's performance seem better than it actually is. A more realistic determination can be found by comparing your child's performance against that of similar children.

• Have the school staff translate the child's performance on these tests into how it reflects on his or her daily functioning in the classroom. This will give you an understanding of how these test results apply to the child's daily educational program, enabling you to understand the practical application of these test results to the child's learning.

• Be careful of "soft soap" words. Listen carefully as the school staff members report the results. You may find that they are not answering your questions directly or seem to be saying one thing and meaning another. At this point, you may have to say: "You don't look happy about these test results. How come?" Or ask, "Are these test results reflective of how my child does in the classroom?" These statement-questions may provide the opening for school staff to fill in the details. If you are told that the test results are not reflective of how your child functions within the classroom, you can request that a note be placed in the records explaining the differences between the child's performance on a test and his or her performance in the classroom. This is important for those who will be looking through these records in the future.

Diagnostic Testing
Diagnostic testing is used to learn specific information about a child in order to explain the child's performance on a screening test or because of the child's performance within the classroom. Diagnostic testing is given to the child individually. Within this individualized testing process, information about how the child learns, inherent weakness in how the child uses and synthesizes information, and possible emotional explanations to explain poor test-classroom performances will be uncovered.

REMEMBER: Before your child can be tested, your permission is required by federal law 94142. You should never receive a surprise phone call that your child will be tested diagnostically. If you do, let school officials know that you will not agree or give permission for testing until you have met with them and determined the intent or purpose of the diagnostic testing. You may want to talk to professionals outside of school before you agree.

While many types of diagnostic tests may be given, it is not important or possible to teach you all there is to know about them. Psychologists disagree over these tests and attribute varying degrees of credibility to the results. That is the main reason why you should not give any more significance to psychological testing (regardless of whether test performances are high or low) than it deserves. You should question school officials about the limitations of the tests.

All diagnostic tests have inherent limitations, and results must be viewed within these limitations. Some tests are more reliable than others. Simply stated, if your child is given the test more than once, the results will be pretty much the same from test to test. Some tests rely on certain methods of information acquisition as opposed to others (e.g., visual acquisition over auditory). Should your child be weak in one area of acquisition compared with another, and the testing methods rely heavily on that area, test results will be lower.

REMEMBER: Diagnostic test results will be aimed primarily at obtaining an intelligence quotient. IQ scores have been stressed as the most important information one can obtain from testing. This is wrong. More important is how your child learns or acquires information. Unfortunately, too many children with "high" IQs never live up to their potential.

The following are important points to remember when considering results of diagnostic testing:

1. The reliability of any individual test increases with the age of the child. The younger the child, the greater the possibility of different results from test to test.
2. IQ is a difficult concept. Simply put, an easier way to understand IQ is to view it as telling you the rate at which your child acquires information. The higher the IQ number, the faster the rate at which the child can acquire information. This does not take into account the time factor. If your child is presented with a certain mount of information, given the child's IQ and enough time to

absorb the information, the child shouldn't have any difficulty. Thus, IQ scores can be misused if they are viewed only as "how smart" a child is as opposed to indicating the rate of acquisition of information. Teachers tend to translate IQ scores into rate of learning when they say: "This is my fast group, or my slow group." You don't hear her saying, "This is my smart group or 'dumb' group." What the teacher is saying is that the fast group can acquire information at a faster rate than the slower group.

3. IQ scores tell you only how much the child has learned up to the time the testing was done. It is not a tool for predicting the total amount of knowledge a child will learn.

The results of such diagnostic testing should help you and the teacher understand your child's learning style, which can be defined as how the child acquires information. Learning styles differ from child to child. Some children have a difficult time learning because they are forced to learn in a way that totally ignores their learning style. The most obvious failure is the learning-disabled child, who, until teachers become aware of the deficiencies, might believe that he or she can't learn rather than understanding that learning must be acquired in a specific, individualized manner.

Test Results
Test results should lead to a better understanding of your child's learning style. This will take into account the rate at which the child learns, the best way to present information to the child, and the strengths and weaknesses of the child's learning processes. Results should develop a hypothesis that will help the child learn more effectively.

REMEMBER: You should have all test results given to you in easily understood, nonjargonistic, everyday common language.

The Test Results Conference
When preparing for the test results conference, you should keep in mind the following points:

● Before the conference, find out who will be in attendance. Some schools feel that everybody from the school principal to the reading specialist should attend. A general rule to follow is that if there are more people at the conference than you want, request only those with whom you wish to speak. Often, these "specialists" won't say something in a large group that they will say to you alone. It is to your advantage to speak to some of these people alone. When planning the conference, ask the following: "Who will attend the conference?" If there are too many, say: "I would like to meet only with Mr. or Mrs. R. I will meet with the others separately."

• Make sure you stress that you do not expect to have someone at the conference whom you did not request. If they show up, you can refuse to meet them. Don't feel embarrassed. It is your child and your right to protect the child's interests.

• Bring your pad and pencil to make notes. Bring a letter with you, requesting a written copy of all test results. Tell the person with whom you are setting up the conference ahead of time that you will want a copy of the test results.

• A clearly defined program to help your child learn more effectively should be outlined by the end of the conference. If there is no clear program for intervention outlined by then, the conference was a waste of your time. Tell the people at the conference: "I'm disappointed that no clear program has been developed for my child. It would seem that all this testing has been a waste of time." Any program presented should be done so in writing, and you should have a copy of it for reference.

• If you feel comfortable with the test results and the program developed, you still may want to think it over. You can say to the school staff at the conference: "I'll have a lot more questions once I get home. Why don't we talk again by phone in the next twenty-four hours before we make any changes." The person with whom you are speaking should say: "I realize I have given you a lot of information. A phone call sounds like a good idea." There is no sense in making a rush decision. If at the conference there appears to be a sense of urgency and a push to get agreement from you before you leave, say: "I don't want to be rushed into any decision today."

• If you are not happy or comfortable with the results of diagnostic testing or feel that your questions have not been fully answered, and you don't understand what has been said, don't become belligerent. Say to the school staff at the conference: "There are a few points I wish to discuss with an outside professional." Obtain a copy of the test results and bring them for a second opinion. You will have to pay for this service, but it is well worth it. To find a psychologist, you can ask the teacher, the pediatrician, the local mental health association, or another parent.

Psychological Testing and Your Child's School Record

Test results will be included in your child's record, and you should know what information is in there. Test results, whether they are from screening tests or diagnostic tests, should be left in your child's record only so long as they provide useful information and are descriptive of the child. Some people feel that none of this information should remain permanently in the school record. If the information is out of the norm, it should be removed if it no longer is useful. The real world remains prejudicial, and information out of the norm that is no longer descriptive of your child may be used against the child many years later.

Keep in mind the following about your child's record and testing:

• Find out who has access to the records. You can request *controlled* access. That means the school has to agree to your request that only certain people can have access to the information provided by the testing.
• Make sure all the language used in the record, especially concerning testing, is understandable. Abbreviations should be coded. If testing material stays in the record, it should be understandable.

POINTS TO REMEMBER

• Always ask: "Will you seek my permission if testing is necessary?" This will help you understand the school's policy concerning testing.
• Educational testing can be used inclusively or exclusively. The former is the only constructive use of such tests.
• Educational testing needs to be translated into a language you understand. Make sure you fully understand the test results before agreeing to program changes.
• Ask for local norms rather than national norms when finding out how your child did on screening tests.

• Diagnostic test results should lead to a better understanding of how your child learns and not simply to an IQ score.

• You should control the conference at which you learn the child's test results. Sometimes more information is given than can be understood, and the presence of too many people can interfere with your ability to understand the results.

• A conference that does not develop an educational program based on diagnostic tests your child has taken should be considered a waste of time.

• Test results should stay in the record only as long as they are descriptive of your child.

• Information about your child that is not within the norm should not be a permanent part of the record.

4

Psychological Needs of Children

Your child may at some time require psychotherapy or counseling. More and more children are receiving these services as the stigma of therapy is being dispelled. Certainly, as parents have become psychologically more sophisticated and social-emotional problems are discussed more openly (in books and on television), the fear of using these services has diminished. Still, society has a long way to go before it permits parents to openly discuss the emotional difficulties of their children without fear of accusation. In previous generations, the general philosophy about children and their critical periods or crises was that they would "outgrow" them. Today, parents, pediatricians, school officials, and family court judges are all well aware that these problems don't just "disappear" but rather require various interventions.

Given the atmosphere in which many children are growing up these days—two full-time working parents, the collapse of the nuclear family (grandparents not living nearby), and the high rate of divorce—the need for professional help seems greater than ever. The assault on the family structure both economically and psychologically is ever increasing. Thus, with the family unit being compromised, children are finding themselves without the necessary psychological supports during the growing-up process. It should come as no surprise that the demand for psychological services for

109

children is increasing and that the individuals and agencies who attempt to meet these demands are trying to keep pace. Unfortunately, quantity does not imply quality. And in the area of psychotherapy and counseling services for children, quality control is almost nonexistent. In parents' frantic desire to do what is best for their children, professionals are chosen haphazardly; while money may be wasted, a greater loss results from the trauma of poorly done therapy. This can forever turn off a child, thus preventing the continuation of therapy in the future and turning possibly minor problems into chronic conditions.

The proliferation of so-called therapies and therapists for children has created a great deal of confusion. Although there is no one way to treat a child's emotional problems, it is important that parents be clear as to the goals and objectives of therapy. Regardless of the orientation of the therapist, whether he or she relies heavily on uncovering the problem (insight-oriented psychotherapy) or changing behavior (behavior management), it is imperative that you be able to maintain open communication with the therapist. Sometimes this communication may be indirect. This occurs with the adolescent in therapy. In order to give adolescents special identity and to maintain their confidence, contact with parents is greatly limited or there is no contact at all. But even in this instance, the decision to progress in this manner is clearly communicated to the parent before the start of therapy, along with a clear explanation for doing it. In that way, although you may not be directly involved in therapy, you have participated in the therapeutic agreement (the contract). In looking for a therapist, it is important that you consider who the person is, the contract for the therapy, and the discipline (whether the therapist is a psychiatrist, psychologist, social worker, etc.).

The Therapist

The success of therapy depends on many things, the most important of which is the relationship between the therapist and the child. Although the circumstances under which the child's difficulties come to light, the duration of the problem, and the emotional status of the family and its individual members are also factors to be considered, the relationship with the therapist is probably the most important. If your child and you can develop a good therapeutic relationship with the therapist, the success of therapy will be much greater. After all, without trust, without feeling that the therapist can help, success is doubtful. You would not consider undergoing heart surgery if you did not have faith and trust in the surgeon. Developing the sense that the therapist is interested in helping you and your child is most important. Feeling that you are just another case does not help to develop the necessary personal touch and interest needed for developing the therapeutic alliance.

It is also important that you sense that the therapist listens to you. Although the therapist will not always agree with what you have to say, and will not necessarily interpret the facts the way you have, it is important that you have the feeling that the therapist is listening to you actively. Active listening implies that the therapist is involved in hearing what you have to say and engages you in such a way as to draw information out. It gives you the impression that the therapist sees your participation in an active way, encouraging it rather than viewing you as a nuisance and an interfering factor in the child's development.

Finding a Therapist
Your child's need for psychological help may come to your attention in any one of a number of ways:

1. The child develops symptoms such as a fear of school or becomes depressed and appears withdrawn and moody. If the symptoms are severe enough, the child, without directly telling you, can be asking for emotional help.
2. The child's behavior becomes a problem; he or she acts out in any one of a number of ways. This can occur at home, disrupting the family, so that the parent seeks help and guidance.
3. The child acts out in school, forcing school authorities to contact you in order to help the child receive psychological care.
4. The child acts out in an antisocial manner that brings him or her in contact with the police or family court. These authorities can suggest psychological help for the child as well as for you. In many situations, the court may order it.

5. The child becomes involved with drugs or alcohol, which often is a sign of underlying emotional problems. The child's impaired functioning may require psychological interventions.

Although I have listed only a few of the many ways a child's need for psychological help may come to a parent's attention, they represent the most frequent ways. Once you realize that your child needs psychological care, you will need to begin the process of looking for a therapist. As we have seen in other chapters, when looking for services for a child, you will rely on the following methods: inheritance, reputation, and recommendation.

Inheritance Method. If you were involved in therapy, you may turn to your own therapist to treat your child. Your therapist most likely will be inappropriate for the child because most adult therapists are neither trained to nor willing to involve themselves with children. Most likely your therapist will suggest alternatives. Assuming that you called your therapist for your child because you trusted the therapist, you can follow his or her recommendations. If the child is in the middle adolescent years (fourteen years and over), the therapist may be willing to become involved since the psychological issues may involve matters he or she is trained to handle.

Reputation Method. Again, this method relies upon who your friends, neighbors, or relatives have used in seeking psychological help for their children. By asking around, you may be surprised that others have sought professional help for their children and have been successful in their attempts. If a particular therapist's name is mentioned positively, you can consider that therapist. Negative reactions to therapists are equally important, especially if they are mentioned repeatedly.

REMEMBER: Don't be misled by what these people have to say. What may have been important to them may not necessarily be important either to you or to the success of your child's therapy.

Recommendation Method. This method, as previously discussed, is based on the recommendation of your pediatrician, guidance counselor, or other professional who knows your child and whom you trust.

In finding a therapist for your child, whether you choose the inheritance, reputation, or recommendation method, you should ask the referring person the following questions:

- "Did you feel that you could talk with the therapist?"
- "Did you meet with the therapist on a regular basis?"
- "Did you feel comfortable with the therapist?"
- "Was the appointment schedule flexible?"
- "Was the therapist available in case of a crisis?"
- "How much did the therapist charge and how did you pay for it?"
- "Did the therapist take a general interest in your child or just limit it to the problems?" It is important that any therapist you choose have a general interest in the whole child, not just in one aspect. A good therapist, regardless of the discipline, should be interested not only in the emotional part of your child's life but also in intellectual and physical growth.
- "How did your child relate to the therapist?" Although it is important to ask this question, it is equally important to keep in mind that a good therapeutic relationship does not necessarily imply that the child like the therapist. The person you are talking with may be able to give you insight into the relationship.
- (If referred by a professional) "Have you referred many children to the therapist?" In asking this question, you are double-checking the referring professional. How the professional responds gives you additional information about how committed he or she is to the therapist.

Initial Contact with the Therapist

If after talking with the referring person you decide to follow through on his or her advice, you will need to make an appointment for your child. At times, others will suggest that they make the appointment for you. Your pediatrician may want to make the appointment, or a family court staffer may wish to do it. You must make the appointment yourself since it will be necessary for you to ask the therapist some important questions. Although you may initially have to talk with a receptionist, most child therapists will want to discuss the matter with you themselves at the time of the initial contact. Should a receptionist attempt to obtain information from you, object by stating: "I would feel more comfortable talking to Dr. P. I'm sure he will want to handle this matter himself." If the therapist doesn't, you should question your choice.

Before the initial phone contact, you should outline for yourself and the therapist your concerns as they regard your child. The therapist will want to obtain a brief outline of the problem.

REMEMBER: Be brief. You'll have plenty of time to go into more detail at the time of the first appointment.

The following are some examples of the problems you might call about in order to receive help:

"My six-year-old son, Tommy, started kindergarten this year. He attended a two-day-a-week nursery school last year. He is an only child and is very close to me (the mother). Getting him ready for kindergarten each morning has been very difficult. He has difficulty waking up, then complains of stomachaches, refuses to get dressed, and cries when the bus comes to get him. I have worked with the teacher to find ways to make it easier for Tommy to get off to school, but it is now three months since school started, and the situation is no better. I feel this problem needs professional help."

"My ten-year-old son, John, for the past six months has been disruptive in class and picking fights at home with his younger brother and sister. John was an average student in the first and second grades, but in the third grade he said the work was 'too hard.' It seemed as if he just stopped working. We feel John was lazy about his schoolwork, and maybe we pressured him more than he could handle about keeping up with his work. By the end of last year, he began to get into trouble in school. At first, his teacher thought it could be handled by us alone, but John told her last week that he felt 'dumb' and 'hated himself.' Now we think the problem is more serious."

"Mary is fifteen. She has always been an obedient girl, did her schoolwork, and was helpful at home. Recently, she has been argumentative with us, has allowed her schoolwork to fall, and seemingly spends all her time talking on the phone with friends. When we try to talk with her, she becomes easily upset, cries, and runs off, saying that we don't understand. We think she needs someone to talk to."

After giving your information, ask, "Is this the type of problem that you deal with?" By saying this to the therapist, you give her the option of refusing to treat your child should she not feel comfortable with the situation. At this point also, the therapist can tell you whether she has time. It is not unusual for there to be a waiting time before your child can be seen. If the therapist cannot see your child immediately (within a week), ask, "Do you think this situation can wait that long?" Obviously, some situations require immediate attention, such as an adolescent suicide attempt. The therapist can advise you and, in fact, begin a therapeutic process by being supportive should she feel that the situation doesn't require immediate attention. If the therapist does not have time to see your child or is unable to see the child as soon as possible, ask the therapist to make a referral. (After all, she was recommended by someone you trusted.) The therapist's referral can be compared with any previous names you obtained when you try a second time.

Fees

If the therapist does not bring up the issue of fees, you must. It is important that therapy not be a financial burden that creates family hardships. Before calling the therapist, you should call your health insurance carrier to determine what benefits you will receive and for whom they will be paid (sometimes insurance reimbursement can be obtained for a psychiatrist but not for a social worker). By knowing how much the insurance company will reimburse you, you can determine whether you can afford private care. (Later in this section we will discuss care provided by public and nonprofit private agencies.) Ask, "How do you expect to be paid?" Some therapists wish to be paid at the time of each visit (especially the first). Others may bill at regular intervals. If therapy is to continue for any length of time, you may be able to work out a contract for payment over a period of time that extends beyond the actual therapy time (paying for therapy after it is finished).

Time

Ask how long a visit lasts. (Most are forty-five to fifty minutes in length.) When you find out, say to the therapist: "If you feel that you will need more time, please feel free to set extra time aside and charge me for it." By stating that, you inform the therapist that you realize it may take longer than usual to discuss your child's problem during the initial visit. This helps the therapist to set aside extra time initially. Some therapists suggest longer initial visits so that the therapeutic process can get under way as soon as possible.

Instruction

Therapists have different approaches for evaluating and treating emotional and behavioral problems. Regardless of the approach, therapy begins with the initial telephone contact. A general rule may be that parents (preferably both) should meet with the therapist without the child initially. In the case of the adolescent, the therapist may wish to meet with the child alone initially. Always ask the therapist why he chooses to meet with you alone or your child alone. If the therapist wants to initiate therapy by meeting with you and the child together (a family approach), it is important that you ask: "How should I approach this matter with my child and what should I say about bringing her to see you?" The therapist should give you some phrases that have been helpful in the past with other children.

REMEMBER: Few children want to go to see a therapist. But if you feel they must, they probably need to. You wouldn't like to be surprised by being told you were going to see a therapist at the last moment. Neither would your child. By telling the child ahead of time, you prevent the therapist from having to deal with greater than normal anxiety.

Having made the initial contact with the therapist, it is important that you begin to organize your thoughts about the child's development. If two parents are involved, both should sit down and make notes. Although different therapists may want to obtain different types of information and will place varying degrees of importance on it, basically all therapists will want to know the following:

• *Information about pregnancy and birth.* Although nine out of ten times information about your pregnancy and the birth and delivery of your child will produce little concrete information relevant to the problem your child is having, it is important that the therapist have a sense of the child's place in the family and know of any possible complications before and during delivery. Failure to ask about your pregnancy may be an important clue to the therapist's limited interest in the whole child. *The therapist should be interested in more than just the problematic parts of your child's life.*

• *Early years and development.* The therapist will want to know about the child's early development along with information about developmental milestones (when the child walked, talked, etc.). In this way, the therapist will begin to put together a longitudinal picture of the child (from past to present). Information concerning the child's physical health is a must. Information concerning illnesses and operations, and especially reactions the child has had to them, is extremely helpful in understanding the child emotionally.

• *Your child's environment.* The therapist will want to develop a picture of the environment(s) in which your child functions. This should include taking a close look at the nuclear family and the extended family (if grandparents, aunts, and uncles play an important role in the child's life). The therapist will want to know about the child's school life, including academic progress, relationships with teachers and schoolmates, and general involvement in school life (athletics, social life, etc.). You should also be able to give a good picture of the child's peer relationships. The environments in which children function are very influential. The therapist needs to have as clear a picture of them as possible. To help you collect facts on these areas, you can organize them to cover the areas depicted in the diagram on page 118.

If you have difficulty describing the child's life in any one of these areas, try to gather more information before visiting the therapist.

Therapy can be compared to a jigsaw puzzle. You and your child will provide the pieces. You, the child, and the therapist will then attempt to fit the pieces together in order to create a picture. Then all of you will attempt to interpret the picture and draw some conclusions that will bring about positive changes in the present behavior and emotional reactions of both you and the child.

In the case of the adolescent, especially the older adolescent, the therapist may wish to see the child without involving you in the initial process. Obviously, it depends on the child's problem. In this

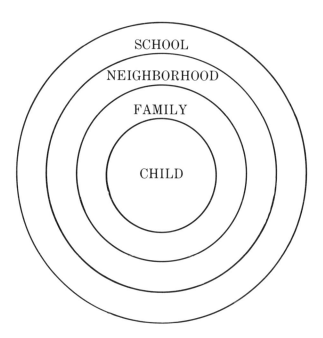

case, the therapist will rely almost totally on the child to provide the information (the pieces of the puzzle). In working with the adolescent, the therapist's greatest initial concern is gaining trust—overcoming the normal suspicions the adolescent has of all adults. The therapist should also want to talk to teachers and other school staff, especially if the problem involves the school environment. You should write down names and phone numbers so that you have the information readily available.

The Initial Visit
At the time of the initial visit to the therapist's office, you will notice not only its appearance but whether it is child-oriented. Does the therapist provide a place for children to entertain themselves (e.g., reading material that is age-appropriate)? This will give you some idea of how the therapist views children and accommodates the office to them. On your first meeting, you will view the therapist in terms of age, sex, and formality. The age of the therapist should

not deter you. Younger therapists are not more "hip" than older therapists. However, the approach or attitude taken by the therapist toward some emotional and behavioral problems may be determined by the therapist's age.

The sex of the therapist has drawn a great deal of attention in psychological journals. Theoretically, all therapists should be able to treat all types of children and problems. However, certain problems may best be treated by a therapist of one sex rather than the other. This is especially true for adolescents, who may find themselves more comfortable talking with a therapist of the same sex. How therapists present themselves and dress projects the degree of formality or lack of it. Although appearances can be deceiving, they often are the first clues to the therapist's personality.

REMEMBER: You are sizing up your child's therapist at the same time that the therapist is looking you over.

The ability of the therapist to put you and your child at ease is extremely important. The therapist should introduce herself to you *and* your child, if the child is present. Failure to introduce herself to the child should raise a question in your mind as to the therapist's general concern and interest in your child.

The therapist at this initial visit will want to gather information concerning you, your child, and the child's environments. You will have brought your notes so that you can provide the necessary history. Therapists have various styles for gathering information. Some allow the parents to set their own pace, directing them to various areas so that all are covered. Others will ask specific questions, leading the parents from area to area. It is important that you feel that you have provided an overall view of the child's development and present functioning. If there is information that you feel the therapist has neglected to gather, say: "I think it is important that you know about. . . ." If the therapist does not respond to this statement, repeat it. A good therapist will not ignore it a second time.

Once you have provided the therapist with the necessary information, you will need to obtain a summary of the problem from the therapist. You should obtain the therapist's view or opinion of the situation, which should include a dynamic picture explaining what is happening and, if possible, how it happened. It is important to remember that the therapist can only draw a picture based on the information obtained from you. However, the therapist puts the facts about your child side by side with his or her experience in other cases and then gives you a professional opinion (for which you are paying). If you have any questions about the picture (formulation) drawn by the therapist, say, "Could you please go over that point again?" or "I'm confused by something you said." Then relate the specific point you want repeated.

You will want to know what role you played in the child's emotional problems. This is one of the more difficult parts of therapy for parents. It is important not to become defensive as the therapist describes your role. The picture should not single you out as the primary cause of the problem. Instead, it should clearly let you know *what part* you played in your child's problem. Except in the case of a young child (under three years), you should not accept one hundred percent of the blame. Obviously, the younger the child, the greater and more complete your influence. As the child grows older, others influence behavior and the child has more ways to react. This is a difficult concept to get across to parents. At times, the wrong therapist will be the one who after hearing the facts sits there berating parents for what they have or haven't done for the child. Such therapists fail to recognize that the parents have made a positive step in seeking therapy for the child and will be turned off by this negative approach.

In the case of the adolescent, the therapist should be able to give you a brief overview of the problem.

REMEMBER: To keep your child's trust, the therapist may not deal with any specific information provided by the child.

However, the therapist should give you enough information so that in determining and defining the therapeutic contract (to be discussed later), you can feel informed enough to be comfortable. *You should not enter into a therapeutic agreement totally blind to the facts and the therapeutic approach.*

The therapist's summary of the problem may appear to be negative. It is important to remember that the therapist draws many conclusions from the negative information presented about the child's problems. However, in looking for solutions to the problem, the therapist should be asking questions about positive aspects of the child, you, and the family. The resolutions for most problems your child and you have lie in the strength of the family's functioning. By knowing the strengths of your child and you, the therapist can begin to define ways of intervening.

A therapist may require that the child have psychological testing, which includes intelligence testing and projective testing (testing that looks closely at the child's emotional functioning). These tests will be discussed in greater detail when we talk about the psychologist as therapist, but for the moment these tests should be viewed as additional ways to understand your child better.

The Therapeutic Contract

The therapeutic contract is the most underestimated and often least looked at part of therapy. Without it, you, your child, and the therapist have no common ground on which to proceed. As the name implies, the therapeutic contract defines the goals of therapy; how therapy is to proceed, including the logistics (such as frequency of visits, payments, etc.) and involvement of you and other members of the family. Let us review each of these points separately:

Goals. Goals of therapy should be defined clearly by the therapist in terms that you understand. This is not the time for psychological jargon but rather for simple, clear statements. An example would be: "Sarah is relying too heavily on you in making everyday decisions. This has become an increasing problem as she becomes an adolescent since she feels a greater need to be more on her own. We have to help her to deal with this conflict, whether to continue to rely on you or break away and become more independent. When we help her figure this out, she'll become less anxious." In this way, you and the child can hear the goals before therapy starts and decide whether the goals are acceptable. If they are not, it is important that you clearly state to the therapist what *your* goals for therapy are: "I was hoping that we could work on. . . ." The therapist should be able to talk about your goals for therapy, include or exclude them from the immediate plan, and give you a reasonable explanation.

REMEMBER: If you and the therapist do not agree on the goals of therapy, therapy will not only be nonproductive and costly but will most likely terminate on a negative note.

Another example of different goals is seen in the typical school-phobic child. As the label implies, the child is believed to be afraid of school or situations found in the school setting. Often such children function outside of school at a level acceptable to the family. Therapists working with these children have learned to look at school phobias as school refusals. The child is not believed to be afraid of school but simply, for a variety of reasons, more comfortable and less anxious staying at home with the parent. The child is brought to the therapist because of the presenting problem of not wanting to go to school. The parent's desire is for the child to return to school as soon as possible. The therapist's desire is usually to have the child return to school but also to recognize the need to explore the relationship of the child within the family.

In this situation, the therapist will want to specifically explore the relationship of the child with the primary caretaking parent. Here, the parents may have one goal while the therapist has a larger goal, realizing that just returning the child to school is being psychologically short-sighted. If this is not fully explained in terms of the goals of therapy, the parents will terminate as soon as the child is "happily" back in school. Furthermore, without a full discussion of goals, exploration of family relationships will seem unrelated to the school phobia. The parents, unaware of the total psychological picture as it concerns the child, may terminate therapy prematurely. The goals of therapy will seem reasonable if the therapist, you, and the child have mapped out together the summary of the problem. Simple logic will almost dictate what needs to be done if the problem is defined clearly.

Fees and Frequency. A further discussion of fees (beyond what was said during the initial telephone call) is necessary. At this point, it is a "fish or cut bait" situation. The therapist has defined the problem and mapped out a course of therapy, and now the first question is one of cost. If you have medical health insurance, you should have checked on your benefits before coming to see the therapist. Some plans pay for psychiatrists but not for social workers. Some have ways of paying for licensed therapists. How much will you have to pay? Few plans pay for the entire bill.

Often, total cost to you depends on how often and for how long your child will have to come to therapy. The therapist will suggest a frequency of therapy: "Jim should come once a week, while I should meet with you once a month." That is a total of about five sessions a month. Ask, "Do you think that the frequency will always be the same as therapy continues?" Most therapists should be able to answer that question by stating that the frequency of therapy is determined by the child's needs. At times, the child may need to be seen more often; as things settle down, the child may need to be seen less often. By stating the question, you at least bring out in the open the fact that you are aware that frequency can change over the course of therapy. One of the most frequent questions is, "How long will therapy last?" Often this question is asked because parents believe that the longer therapy takes, the worse the problem(s). The therapist is likely to reply that it is difficult to put an exact time limit on therapy. However, the therapist should be able to give you a general figure based on previous experiences. Having determined frequency of visits and the fee, you must decide whether you can afford therapy.

It is not a good idea to start therapy and see how long your money can last. To stop therapy midway is similar to stopping a blood transfusion halfway through the bottle. In fact, stopping therapy is worse since it leaves a great deal of angry feelings in all concerned parties.

If money is a problem, discuss this issue with the therapist. If another referral needs to be made, this is the time to do it. The therapist should be able to help you in this matter. You have not wasted your time, as you have received an expert opinion about the nature of the problem and ways to resolve it.

Parental Involvement. At this point during the initial contact, the therapist may make two separate appointments. In that case, the logistics of therapy may be discussed after the second meeting. Your involvement should be discussed. Does the therapist want you to be involved on a regular basis (e.g., half the visit with your child, the other with you alone or with your child and you)? If the therapist does not involve you, ask the following: "Can you explain to me why you do not feel we should be directly involved our child's therapy?" The therapist should give you clear reasons for exclusion. Other than for adolescents, exclusion of parents should be for very strong reasons. The counterpart to this is if the therapist recommends that both parents or one parent should be seen in therapy without the child. In this case, the therapist has detected problems above and beyond the child, which if treated will benefit the child, even though the child is not directly involved in therapy. On occasion, although your child may have provided the reason for seeking help, it may soon become apparent that you need direct help for yourself.

It is important that you discuss with the therapist ways of communicating information to each other, especially in a crisis. Does the therapist mind being called after hours? Can you call before a session if you feel that the therapist needs additional new information? How will the therapist let you know of any new important changes in the child? Ask the therapist: "What kinds of information would you like to know about? How should we go about communicating it?" This is an important question. Some therapists may want to have all information about the child discussed in front of the child. Others, for equally valid therapeutic reasons, may prefer to have you communicate via the telephone before any session rather than taking time away from the child's session. *Discuss this openly.*

Drugs and Hospitalization. Drugs, specifically tranquilizers and stimulants (for the treatment of the "hyperactive" child), can be a part of the treatment. Ask the therapist: "Do you see any need for medication?" Except for psychiatrists, other therapists by law cannot prescribe medication. However, given their experience in working with children, they should be knowledgeable about problems that may be treatable with medication. They often will use a child psychiatrist or pediatrician to work with them in prescribing appropriate medication.

In the present climate, the use of medication is generally considered a "bad" thing. When medication is suggested as an adjunct to therapy, parents quickly conjure up visions of their children in a trancelike, zombie state. This comes about through the terrible misinformation provided to the general public and from frequently repeated horror stories about individual children. There is no doubt that in some instances medication for children has been misused. At times, it has been prescribed as a "first resort" before other therapeutic interventions have been tried or allowed to work.

The use of tranquilizers and other drugs in the treatment of children has both its limitations and its drawbacks. The predictability of responses to these medications in children is highly variable. In fact, for some children on these drugs, the response can be the opposite of what is expected. Discuss with the therapist any possible use of medications. Ask: "Why are you considering (or would you consider) using medication?" The therapist should give you clear reasons for using any medication and describe the anticipated effects. These described effects should complement the overall goal of therapy. Often, medication is used on a child not so much for the needs of the child as for the needs of parents, teachers, etc. *Make sure the medication is being prescribed because your child needs it, not because you or the school feels it's necessary.*

It is very important that you clearly understand the side effects of the medication. Side effects at times may become so great as to prevent further use of the drug. Find out how you can talk to the therapist should there be a change in your child that you think is attributable to the drug's side effects. For some drugs, it may be suggested that the child have some baseline blood work. These drugs, like any drugs, can produce harmful effects on the body, which can show up as changes in the blood. Baseline blood work is an excellent precaution and should be obtained before the drug is started.

It is also important that you set up with the therapist a system whereby you can discuss any changes in dosage. Often a drug doesn't have the desired effect because it wasn't prescribed at a high enough dosage level. Ask: "How do you want me to let you know about any problems with the medication?" The therapist should reply that you can discuss medication between sessions. If the therapist doesn't, you should say: "I'm not comfortable waiting until the next session if my child's medication is not under control."

It is important that you also ask: "How long do you think the child will be on medication?" This is both a fair and an unfair question. Although the therapist may not be able to (and probably shouldn't) give an exact time limit, he should be able to give you an answer that shows that he views the use of medication as part of the overall treatment plan rather than *the* treatment plan. The therapist may reply by saying: "I plan on using it until your child gets over this present high state of anxiety." The therapist may explain to you that medication may be needed on and off, depending on the functioning (or lack of it) of the child. This may also explain future dosage changes.

This conversation with the therapist is very important. All too often, sudden use of medication, stopping of medication, or increased dosage can be misinterpreted by parents to mean some change, good or bad, in therapy. In fact, it may have just the opposite significance.

Residential Placement. Hospitalization of a child under twelve for emotional or behavioral problems is unusual but not rare. In the adolescent age range, the use of a residential placement (out of the home) is more frequent. Determine whether the therapist foresees any use of a residential placement. This can include hospitalization or placement in an overnight facility (e.g., a residential school). Placement for any reason is a serious matter since it disrupts the family and removes the child from the home. However, at times, in order to gain additional time for your child and to give the child a more neutral environment in which to function (especially if the negative interactions have gotten out of hand at home or in school), placement becomes mandatory. If you talk about the situation ahead of time, should the need arise, it will not come as a surprise. Furthermore, it also allows the parent the opportunity to bring up the matter in the future should the need arise.

Therapy is a process that seldom has room for unilateral decisions (decisions made by the therapist alone or by you alone). Successful therapy is founded on mutual trust between the therapist, the child, and the parent. Decisions to begin, change, and terminate therapy are reached after careful discussion of the conscious (and at times unconscious) reasons. To act unilaterally—the therapist alone, your child alone, or you alone—is a destructive maneuver that in no way helps the child. Any discussion of termination of therapy must include a review of the initial therapeutic contract and the goals of therapy. If there is mutual agreement that some or all of these goals have been achieved, termination would seem appropriate.

If You're Unhappy with Therapy

Often your child or you will become unhappy with how therapy is progressing. You may feel that the child's behavior is not changing fast enough or that some of the child's actions are getting "worse."

It is important that you and the therapist have discussed ways in which you can communicate these concerns. It should be a part of any therapeutic contract that periodically your child and you or you alone can sit down with the therapist in order to assess and reassess the goals and progress of therapy. If you are unhappy with the therapy, say to the therapist: "I'm concerned about my child in therapy. I think we need to go over our goals for her again." A good therapist will understand your concern and be willing to discuss it with you. If you are feeling that you would rather not return to the therapist, don't act arbitrarily. If you and the therapist cannot resolve the problem, at least discuss it openly and hear the therapist out. Abruptly leaving is not only untherapeutic to your child but costly.

POINTS TO REMEMBER

Checklist for rating your child's therapist

☐ Is the therapist interested in all of your child's development or just social-emotional growth?

☐ Does the therapist appear to take an active interest in your child or is your child just "another case?"

☐ Does the therapist listen to you and your child?

☐ Do you feel that you can relate to the therapist?

☐ Does the therapist explain things in language you and the child can understand, or are things explained in psychological jargon?

☐ Do you understand the therapeutic contract, including:

☐ the child's problem

☐ the goals of therapy

☐ the logistics of therapy, including cost and time

☐ present or potential use of medication and residential hospital placement

If you can respond yes to all of the above, you have probably been able to find an appropriate therapist who will help your child's social-emotional development. The next sections are devoted to giving you a better understanding of the types of therapists one can choose from. There will be pros and cons to your choice, but an *informed* choice will help your child.

The Psychologist

You probably have a general understanding of the role of a psychologist. There seems to be less confusion about this role than about the roles of the child psychiatrist and the social worker. You may already know that psychologists work with "psychological problems" and "do testing." Beyond that, the picture becomes vague.

A child psychologist should be able to treat most kinds of childhood and adolescent problems. As the title implies, the child psychologist should have had additional and specialized training in the area of childhood and adolescent development. Although all psychologists have had some training experience with children, it is important to know what additional training they have had in this area. If you are referred to a *clinical* child psychologist, you can assume that the therapist has had additional training in working with and understanding children and is interested in this area of work. A general psychologist may only have a passing interest in children. Thus, when your child is being referred to a psychologist for either psychological testing or therapy, ask: "Has Dr. R. had special training with children or is she a general psychologist?" The referring person should be able to tell you about the child psychologist's credentials. If he or she can't, you should think twice about using this recommendation.

Psychologists in general are referred to as "Doctor." At times, there is confusion between the Ph.D. and the M.D. Child psychologists do not go to medical school. However, after college, they receive training at least at the Master's level and additional training to receive a doctorate. It is important to remember that the psychologist may or may not have received a doctorate in work done with children. In general, however, the fact that the psychologist has a Ph.D. implies specialized training and thus competency. Most states license psychologists who wish to carry on a private practice. In this way, there is a minimum acceptable standard by which psychologists can perform their duties.

Therapists, psychologists, child psychiatrists, and social workers can all use a similar theoretical framework. The formal and informal training does not preclude the use of any one of the many therapeutic options available. If you tend to view psychologists as professionals who work only on a child's behavior, you have a very common although misguided idea about how they work. Psychologists can be viewed in general as trying to figure out what makes a personality. Thus, if a child psychologist is seeing your child, he or she would try to understand what makes up the child's personality, what the symptomatic problems that the child is having are, and how they fit into the child's overall personality pattern. In doing this, the child psychologist can attempt to figure out ways of changing the child's behavior (getting rid of the symptoms).

Fortunately, the child psychologist's view of children is broader than that one aspect. The child psychologist should be more than just a behavior modifier. There are child psychologists who simply see themselves as changers of children's behavior and show little interest in general functioning. This is being very short-sighted, and working with such an individual may have immediate but limited gains. In the long run, you may be selling your child short. Although treating symptoms can be of value at times, it fails to get at the root of the problem(s); it is much like treating a fever with aspirin and never finding out what is causing the fever.

Child psychologists are specifically trained in the administration of psychological tests to children and adolescents. Elsewhere, we have discussed educational testing, or ways of understanding how a child learns. Child psychologists can give you general information about a child's intellectual functioning. The psychological testing can give important and necessary information about the child's social-emotional functioning that might not otherwise be obtainable. Later in this chapter, we will discuss in greater detail psychological testing as it applies to the child.

Finding a Child Psychologist

The ways in which your child will be referred to a child psychologist differ little from other ways in which the child was previously referred for services. Guidance counselors in school can be a major referral source. When talking to the guidance counselor or anyone else making the referral, ask the following: "Has Dr. R. had success with this type of problem?" By asking this question, you should be able to get additional information about the person with whom your child will be working. Many times, the child may be referred to a child psychologist because of a need for psychological testing. Ask the referring individual: "Have you used this psychologist often for psychological testing?" By asking this question, you are letting the referring individual know that you want as much information as you can obtain about this psychologist before you will allow your child to be seen. Basically, the methods for finding a child psychologist are the same as for finding other professionals.

Psychological Testing

Before we proceed, it is important that you understand why your child may need psychological testing. Certainly, if the recommendation is made to you by the school or by the child's pediatrician or any other professional, they should be able to explain in a clear manner why the referral is necessary.

Psychological testing is a valuable aid in better understanding the emotional and intellectual functioning of a child. Only in a rare instance should it be used as a blanket approach to gaining information. The value of psychological testing is greatly increased when the referring individual asks specific questions that the testing can attempt to answer. Such questions include: "How good is his judgment?" "How does she view herself when compared to friends?" "Does he suffer from a depression deeper than what we see?"

These are important and serious questions, but they are specific questions. The value of psychological testing is lost if the referring individual uses the testing process as a "fishing trip," not knowing what he or she is looking for but hoping for some answers. Psychological testing should supply additional answers to questions for which the referring individual already has some answer from a clinical assessment. Most of the time, psychological testing should give additional answers, not new questions. Thus, we can view psychological testing and its value in the following way:

1. Psychological testing is useful for determining the severity of a child's emotional problem. It can give information that may help the therapist in deciding the type of interventions the child can handle emotionally as well as knowing whether the more serious underlying problems could be precipitated by stresses associated

with certain therapeutic interventions when compared with others. The psychological tests that help give these types of answers are called projective tests. They tend to be unstructured tests. That means that the test material can have many answers rather than a right or wrong answer. It allows the child, for instance, to look at a picture of a scene (e.g., a parent and child talking), and then tell a story about the picture. Your child's answer(s) can give clues to inner thoughts that may not be accessible through the question-answer format.

2. Psychological testing can provide additional information about your child's intellectual functioning (IQ). This testing can help the therapist understand the child's present level of intellectual functioning and compare it with previous tests. It also gives some basis for determining the child's intellectual potential. IQ testing can at times show discrepancies between one area of intellectual functioning and another. This testing is most useful should your child be functioning at a previously unrecognized below-normal level; such a problem could be a major contributor to the child's sense of worthlessness. (A poor school performance contributes to a low self-image.) Furthermore, if this testing does reveal mental retardation or less-than-normal intellectual functioning, it will most likely lead to additional testing (educational testing) in order to help the child have more successful educational growth.

3. At times, psychological testing is helpful in determining whether the child has an organic (physical) or neurological impairment. This may be helpful in understanding children with minimal brain dysfunction or hyperactivity. Explaining your child's overactive behavior on the basis of an organic cause allows for a different intervention than if the overactivity is ascribed to a primary emotional problem and related to increased anxiety.

4. Should your child be essentially nonverbal (as in the case of a very shy and withdrawn child), psychological testing, both projective and intellectual, may be crucial to a full and better understanding and thus to more appropriate intervention(s). For some children, verbal communication is a slow and painful process. The knowledge gained through psychological testing may help the child overcome this hurdle and aid in the child's growth and development.

It is important to stress the point that in asking for your child to have psychological testing, the individual referring the child should not do so with the instructions, "Give the child the battery of tests." If the referral is done in this manner, the referring individual has little knowledge of psychological testing and its usefulness. Basically, he or she is going on a fishing expedition with your child as bait. What they are really saying is, "Give the child the tests, and let's see what we find." Rather, the referring individual should ask specific questions that help the psychologist decide the kinds of tests the child should have.

Before your child has psychological testing, the following should happen:

1. The psychologist should want to meet with you beforehand. If he or she doesn't, you should ask: "Wouldn't you like to meet with us first?" If the psychologist says no, say that you'll call back and recontact the referring individual. There is a real problem with this type of psychologist.

2. When meeting with the psychologist, ask: "Do you do all your own testing?" If the psychologist says no, ask why. It is not to your child's advantage to be tested by someone else and then have the psychologist read the results. Much happens at the time of testing that a good child psychologist will want to see directly and not hear secondhand from someone else.

3. Ask the psychologist: "What tests or types of tests are you going to give my child?" The psychologist should be able to give you a clear understanding of the tests in everyday language. Ask: "Would it be possible for me to see some examples?"

4. Ask the psychologist: "How will we learn about the results?" If the psychologist says he or she will send you a report, ask: "Then you don't plan on helping us understand the results?" This should put the psychologist on notice that you expect to have meetings (and pay for the time) so that he or she can fully explain the child's tests and answer all your questions. You will want to know such things as where the child's anxiety is coming from and what factors (you, school, or other important parts of the environment) are contributing.

5. Ask the psychologist to tell you about the reliability of the tests applied. It is important to remember that there are many types

of tests used to understand a child's level of intellectual functioning and to determine the child's emotional functioning. Various testers rely on certain tests. Ask: "Have you found these tests to be reliable?"

Different tests provide different data. However, the data should provide a general picture. Any one test that provides information that is very different from all the others should be looked at with suspicion. Various psychological tests act as checks and balances for one another. *No one test can tell it all.* You can ask: "What test(s) did you rely on most?"

For example, your child may have taken a sentence-completion test in which the tester gives the child a sentence that the child finishes. The sentence-completion test may show that the child has a low self-opinion. On projective testing (for instance, telling stories about pictures shown to the child), the child may give a pattern of response that shows depression. Finally, on achievement testing, the child may demonstrate poor concentration. All these answers are consistent. Each test essentially provides data that back up the other tests.

6. Psychological tests do not constitute answers in and of themselves. If the psychologist says that the testing will tell you "what's wrong," you should be very suspicious. This type of promise can be not only misleading but destructive to the child.

7. Be concerned about computer scoring of the test results. This should tell you that the tester is relying not on personal observations and experience but on a machine and standardized responses (statistics only).

8. If the child is receiving psychological testing to determine intellectual functioning and present level of achievement, ask the psychologist: "Will you make a school visit after you test her?" If the psychologist says no, state: "We are willing to pay for that service." If the tester intends only to send a report, you should say: "I think I need to think this over and will contact you later." If you ask this question at the time of the initial phone contact, hang up and don't call back. If you find this out during the initial visit, reconsider your choice. The value of psychological testing in this type of situation is the ability of the psychologist to help translate the results of the psychological testing to teachers and other school personnel. Failure to make the school visit tells you

that this psychologist has a limited view of his or her role. *You will be wasting your money and not helping your child if the psychologist does not have direct contact with the school.*
9. Ask the psychologist how you should prepare the child for testing. You can tell the child: "You will be taking some fun tests where there are no right or wrong answers. There are other tests that will remind you of school, but unlike school, you don't get any grades."

When your child has been tested, you will want a full report (copy) and a full understanding and explanation of the report in simple language. You should ask the psychologist: "What does this report tell you about my child?" If the report is to be shared with others (e.g., school), you should discuss with the psychologist the necessity of writing a summary, especially for projective testing. You should ask: "I'm concerned that your report or any labels used to describe my child may be misunderstood. How can we prevent that?"

REMEMBER: Make sure the psychologist satisfies you on this point. Many a report or label has been used against a child rather than in the child's favor.

Behavioral Interventions

A point should be made about behavior modification and other interventions that attempt to change a child's behavior at the symptom level without dealing directly with the underlying emotional conflicts. A good behavioral approach requires a good history of the child. Without it, the therapist obtains a one-sided and limited view of the child and family. Psychologists receive formal training in behavioral techniques. The other practitioners (child psychiatrist and social worker) all use behavioral interventions in their therapy as well. But many times referrals are made to psychologists in the belief that they can set up a "behavioral contract" for helping the child and you resolve the problem.

If you and the child become involved in a behavioral program, it is important to remember that often it is not enough. The more severe underlying problems are not always so easily resolved by changing one behavior or even two. That is not to say that there is no value in approaching a child in terms of behavioral interventions, but it would be naive to view such an approach as a panacea. The psychologist should view behavioral techniques as one of a number of ways to approach the child therapeutically. Should the therapist begin to talk about behavior modification, ask: "How does this behavioral intervention fit in with other types of psychological help for my child?" "Do you feel that it is important that we try to figure out *why* the child feels and acts this way?" If the psychologist shows little further interest in discovering the underlying emotional dynamics of the child's behavior, reconsider using him or her as your child's therapist.

Social Workers

Social workers are trained to work with parents and children, although there are obvious differences that set them apart from child psychiatrists and child psychologists. If your child is referred to a social worker for therapy, you will want to know a number of pieces of information. Ask specifically: "What training have you had with children?" Although this appears to be a simple question, it can be very revealing. A social worker working with your child should be a M.S.W. (Master's in Social Work), which means that this individual has had training in social work beyond the college level and should have had a good deal of clinical training (actual work with families and children). The social worker should be licensed by the state. Once again, a license is no guarantee of quality. Rather, it sets a minimum standard.

Social workers, except those few with special training, do not involve themselves in psychological testing. On occasion, they may use an abbreviated version of one of the tests to obtain a quick understanding about a child concerning a specific point (e.g., intellectual functioning). Social workers, however, are not trained to do formal testing. When you set up the therapeutic contract, you can discuss with the social worker what will be done if psychological testing is necessary. The social worker should be able to tell you how he or she makes referrals to a psychologist if necessary.

Social workers are not physicians and cannot prescribe medication. However, in the course of treatment, a social worker may feel that your child requires medication. At the time of setting up the therapeutic contract, ask: "What will you do if you think my child needs medication?" The social worker should be able to tell you whether he or she refers to a specific child psychiatrist or to the child's pediatrician. The two of you should reach a mutual agreement at this time as to how this intervention would be carried out and with whom.

Social workers tend to view children therapeutically as part of the family unit. Although some social workers are trained to feel comfortable working with children in individual therapy, most will view your child and the accompanying social-emotional problems within the dynamics of the family. Thus, the social worker will spend a great deal of time trying to understand you. At times, it will seem that the social worker is focusing on the wrong member of the family, you rather than the child. The social worker will also obtain a good history of the child.

If you feel that the social worker is spending too much time finding out information about you, ask: "It seems that you are spending all your time talking about me (or us). Is this going to help my child?" The social worker should be able to give you a clear explanation as to why information is being gathered in this manner. He or she will also be greatly interested in the child's environment outside the home: specifically, school, neighborhood, and community. The social worker will want to find out as much as possible about your child's interactions in these various "life spaces" and how the child functions in them. To do this, it is important to ask the social worker: "You have asked a great deal about my child's school. Do you plan on finding out more about it?" The social worker should respond by saying: "If necessary, I would like your permission to call the teacher (or principal or guidance counselor) and possibly visit if necessary."

At times, you may be concerned about school personnel finding out that your child is being seen in therapy. Most schools understand that children and their parents may need professional help to resolve emotional conflicts. In fact, knowledge of your child's involvement may help them help the child and give them some explanations of why the child behaves a certain way in certain situations. Furthermore, at times during the course of therapy (regardless of who is providing it), your child may have a variety of reactions, some of which can be negative (and often only temporary). Keeping school personnel informed may help them ease the pressure on the child and allow for appropriate therapeutic responses to the child's behavior (rather than, for example, sending the child to the principal's office for being a nuisance).

REMEMBER: A well-trained social worker provides more than just counseling (formal advice). A social worker should provide therapy: an ability to understand the underlying dynamics of the child and the family and to interpret the facts in a way that allows for positive change among all family members.

As with other therapists, you will have to discuss fees. At the time of the initial phone call, discuss fees and the type of payment. Although third-party payment (health insurance) is allowed in some states for coverage of therapy by social workers, it is still not available nationwide. Furthermore, the amount that an insurance carrier will reimburse a social worker can vary greatly from what is provided for services by other professionals. Your decision not to use the services of a fully trained social worker may be based on the fact that you cannot afford it because your insurance won't provide coverage or adequate reimbursement.

POINTS TO REMEMBER

• Social workers provide more than just counseling. If properly trained, they provide psychotherapy.

• Social workers tend to look at children within the context of the family and the environment rather than taking a direct view of the child; they are not usually trained to work in individual therapy with children. Before starting therapy, find out how the social worker plans to treat your child. If you remain uneasy about the child not being seen in individual therapy, ask: "Do you think my child needs to be seen in individual therapy?" The social worker should be able to give you a clear and reasonable response.

Child Psychiatrists

As therapists, child psychiatrists bring to the therapeutic situation not only their psychological training but their background as licensed physicians. Because of this, their understanding of the child can be greater in such areas as physical growth and development as well as in diagnosing behavioral problems when it is unclear whether the cause is primarily emotional or physical. This can be very important when deciding which therapist to pick. Many times, a child's problems will involve not only an emotional upheaval but also somatic complaints. This is commonly seen in the child who uses headaches as a way of dealing with anxiety and unconsciously manipulates the environment to avoid a stressful situation. Therapists who have a limited understanding of organic illness and associated symptoms will feel in a more compromised position when attempting to resolve the problem of "psyche" (emotional) versus "soma" (body).

The child psychiatrist has received training as a physician and has received training after medical school in both adult and child psychiatry. Besides having to be licensed to practice as a physician in your state, the child psychiatrist may also be certified in adult psychiatry and neurology and may have certification in child psychiatry. The additional certification is provided by the American Psychiatric Association and the American Academy of Child Psychiatry. Although this certification demonstrates a certain proficiency to practice psychiatry and work with parents and children in a therapeutic situation, it is important to remember that these examinations fail to test for the ability of the therapist to relate to you and your child.

It is worth asking the child psychiatrist if he or she is board-certified. If not, it can be a factor in your decision to use this psychiatrist to help you work with your child. Adult psychiatrists, by training, have had little experience with children. Unlike child psychiatrists, who have had at least two years of specialty training working with children and adolescents, adult psychiatrists usually have had limited exposure.

When you are referred to a therapist who is identified as a child psychiatrist, it is very important to make sure the therapist *is* a child psychiatrist. There are very few child psychiatrists practicing in the United States when compared with the number of adult psychiatrists. Many adult psychiatrists will be uncomfortable enough to inform you at the time of the initial telephone call that they limit their practice to adults. Others may not. Many adult psychiatrists feel comfortable working with teenagers rather than children.

Whether you are talking with a child psychiatrist or an adult psychiatrist, ask the following: "What is your experience working with adolescents and children?" If the adult psychiatrist replies that he or she works a great deal with children your child's age or has had special training with this age group, you may want to wait and meet the therapist before passing judgment. In general, however, child psychiatrists have had special training with all children. Their understanding of the growth and development of children from infancy to eighteen years should be complete. One generally cannot say this about adult psychiatrists.

There are immediately apparent differences between the child psychiatrist and other therapists. First of all, as previously stated, the child psychiatrist is a licensed physician, thus bringing to the therpautic situation knowledge of how organic and psychological illness interact. He or she has the ability to define behavioral problems created by psychological factors as opposed to those brought about by a physical component. In obtaining a developmental history, the psychiatrist calls forth previous experience from training in pediatrics, obstetrics, and other specialties. The psychiatrist has the ability to view your child in a broader light simply because of his or her medical background. He or she may be the first professional that your child comes in contact with who will be asked to answer the question: "Is my child involved with a primarily psychological problem or is there a physical cause?"

An example of this is seen in the confusing picture of the "hyperactive" or minimally brain dysfunctional child. Such children are seen as suffering from increased motor activity, poor attention span, and occasional clumsiness caused by a neurological problem. The distinction between a "hyperactive" child and an "overactive" child (not neurologically based) can at times be made only by a professional with both a medical and a behavioral background. That is not to say that other nonmedical therapists cannot make equally good professional assessments. It means that a child psychiatrist is better prepared to make these as well as other evaluations.

Medication and Hospitalization
Only a licensed physician can prescribe medication to your child. Of the three therapists described, only a child psychiatrist can prescribe medication. Thus, it is extremely important when forming

the therapeutic contract with the psychiatrist that you specifically ask: "Do you use drugs in the treatment of children?" The therapist should answer your question clearly and to the point. You should state: "If you decide that medication will help my child, I hope that you will discuss that decision with us ahead of time." This statement informs the therapist that you expect to be involved in such an important decision.

REMEMBER: Medication and the use of it for your child is a serious matter; you must be involved and fully informed.

Whenever the child psychiatrist prescribes medication, he or she must be able to answer the following questions:

1. *Why is the medication being prescribed?* It is very important to understand why the therapist feels that medication will help your child. The therapist should be able to clearly state the goals of medication and what he or she hopes to achieve. At times, it may simply be a prescription of a nighttime sedative for a child who is fearful of the dark and has been unable to sleep. Whatever the situation, it is important that you understand the reasons so that whether the medication works or not, you can discuss the situation with the therapist.

2. *How long will the child be on medication?* This question is closely tied into the answer to the first question. Obviously, your child will be on medication only as long as is necessary. In some situations, children are placed on tranquilizers to help them through a particularly difficult time. Others may be placed on tranquilizers to lessen their anxiety in a chronic situation. It is important that you understand the time frame.

3. *What are the side effects?* All medications, including aspirin, have side effects. The types of medication most often used for children have side effects that you must understand. You should ask: "Tell me the specific effects I should look for." You should be aware of these side effects so that you can be of help should the therapist wish to change from one medication to another or change the dosage. Furthermore, some medications have initial side effects that are annoying but not critical. These may have to be explained to your child so that he or she will not be frightened. It may initially be required that the child have blood tests because some

medications can alter body functions, which is first seen in changing blood values. Again, this is not to be considered a reason against the use of medication but rather a precautionary measure.

The expected and desired effect of medication for children, especially children under twelve, is not as predictable as in the case of adults. Thus, children need to be monitored more closely. Also, because children are in the process of growing and their nervous systems are not fully mature, the long-term effects of chronic drug use are not fully understood. When prescribing medication, the child psychiatrist should tell you: "I want to talk with you weekly about your child and the child's medication, especially until we adjust the dose and see how the child reacts to the medication." "Should there be any *sudden* changes in the child's behavior, I want to know immediately. It may mean that we have to change the dosage or the medication."

The child psychiatrist should not say: "Try the medication, and we will talk about it in two weeks." If he implies that he may not be readily available to talk about the medication, ask: "Would medication be best handled by our pediatrician?" This arrangement can be worked out between the psychiatrist and pediatrician. Since the pediatrician has an on-call system that is readily available, she or her associates may be more available should you have questions about the medication. The pediatrician should be informed immediately if your child is taking medication prescribed by the child psychiatrist. That way, if she treats your child for any childhood illness, she doesn't treat the child for something that may be drug-related or prescribe medication that is incompatible with the medication already being taken.

On occasion, your child may need hospitalization for psychological problems. This may be seen in the suicidal adolescent or the child who is severely acting out. These hospitalizations will most often occur on an emergency basis, given that there is a facility willing to hospitalize the "emotionally disturbed child." Under these circumstances, the child psychiatrist is the only one of the therapists described to have hospital privileges. By having the child psychiatrist provide therapy and hospitalization, continuity of care is ensured. This is a vital factor at a most difficult time.

A word is necessary here about psychological testing by child psychiatrists. Many parents are confused about the difference between a child psychologist and a child psychiatrist. In the area of psychological testing, the confusion can return if you do not understand the following points. Child psychologists spend a *good part* of their training learning how to give and interpret psychological tests. Child psychiatrists, as *part of* their training, *may* learn how to give some psychological tests. Ask: "Do you give psychological tests or do you use a child psychologist?" This should show the therapist that you know the difference between the two disciplines and understand that a child psychologist, in most instances, is the more appropriate professional to formally test a child psychologically. If the therapist does perform these tests, ask: "If you find something on your tests, will you have my child tested by a psychologist?" This reinforces your desire to have your child tested, if necessary, by a professional trained in the formal testing of children and adolescents.

Child Psychiatrists as Therapists

As part of his or her training, a child psychiatrist is exposed to a variety of clinical settings, types of children, and therapies. A good training program should expose the psychiatrist to the various developmental problems of children and adolescents, including not only the primary emotional difficulties but also learning disorders, mental retardation, and neurological impairment. When discussing your child with the child psychiatrist, after the psychiatrist has a clear understanding of the problem, ask: "Do you work often with children like mine?" This helps to address the comfort and experience the psychiatrist has with these types of problems. For instance, many child psychiatrists have had little training or experience working with mentally retarded children and their families. Therapeutic approaches to these types of situations, as well as interest and commitment, can vary. Find out ahead of time.

REMEMBER: Therapists, regardless of their background, have particular interests and enjoy certain types of children's problems more than others. It is important to determine this ahead of time.

The child psychiatrist, of the three types of therapists, usually has had the most formal training working directly with children in therapy, most often referred to as "play therapy." If the psychiatrist relates to you that your child will be seen in play therapy, you should ask: "Can you tell me what you will be doing with the child in play therapy?" The therapist should be able to give you a clear understanding of what play therapy involves. The following are the essential functions of play therapy.

1. For the preschool and early-latency-age child (up to ten or eleven years), play therapy allows the child to deal with emotionally conflictual situations in an indirect way. Rather than identifying the problem and discussing it with the therapist, the child can deal with the problem indirectly, through play. Although "indirect" may sound misleading, it still allows the child an opportunity to resolve the conflict. Within the play setting, the child can develop various play themes, and this allows the child to discharge the emotional energy connected with the situation. For instance, in the situation of a child who is angry that a newborn sibling apparently has displaced him or her within the family setting, the child can, through play, act out the fantasized destruction of the younger sibling, can be given permission for these feelings, can be helped to understand the jealousy, and can realize how to find restitution within the new family setting.

2. Play therapy allows the child, along with the therapist, to unravel the conflicts that may not initially be seen during the diagnostic process. The use of the term "diagnostic process" as opposed to "therapy" is misleading. Any diagnostic process can give you only a certain limited amount of information. Therapy continues the diagnostic process as more and more information is learned. Thus, play allows this process to continue as well as helping your child work through the conflict and find emotionally satisfying and therapeutic solutions. Your child's personality becomes clearer, and this helps the therapist understand the elements outside of the child that have contributed to the child's present psychological functioning.

3. Play therapy can be a dress rehearsal for dealing with life situations that have not yet been mastered. For the school-phobic youngster, playing out the emotional trauma of leaving home to go to school can ease the pain of the real thing and allow for a direct discussion of the anxiety.

4. Play therapy allows therapists to view children in a number of different roles. First, it allows the child to obtain a picture of his or her self-image. Second, the child has an opportunity to com-

municate thoughts and feelings about the person engaging him in play and his view of the therapist. Finally, in play, the child will treat the therapist in ways he treats other significant people in his life, such as parents. These are called "transference reactions," and seeing them allows the therapist the opportunity to better understand faulty interactions between the child and others.

Play therapy provides a valuable therapeutic tool for some children. Not all children benefit from play therapy, and it is erroneous to feel that if your child is not seen in play therapy, he or she is not being treated properly. Play therapy has value if its purpose is viewed as providing a setting in which more can be understood about the child rather than as a cure-all. In discussing play therapy with the psychiatrist, it is important to ask how the information the therapist learns about your child will be shared with you.

Many times, therapists enter into confidentiality agreements with children, giving a promise that no information or communication between child and therapist will be shared with the parents. This is an inappropriate and often untenable arrangement. There will be times when it is very important that *some* information be shared with the parents. Sometimes this will help to ensure the continued safety and welfare of the child. To have entered into such a prior confidentiality pact will jeopardize the trust of the child in the therapist should the agreement have to be broken. It is unusual for a child or adolescent not to reach some agreement with the therapist, even if on a limited basis, for sharing information with parents.

One final word about play. At times it will appear as if you were paying a therapist just to play with your child. It will seem from your child's account that the play is repetitious, and it will sound as if therapy were getting you and your child nowhere. At times, play therapy *seems* to go on endlessly and without results. However, many times, the working through of the problem is a slow process and is not always directly observable, as in the case of a wound healing or a rash becoming smaller in size. It is appropriate for you to ask the therapist: "How is my child's play therapy relating to her psychological problem?" The therapist should be able to share with you as much information as he or she has been able to gather and relate it to the child's functioning. In the therapeutic contract, this type of information sharing should be agreed upon by you and the therapist before therapy starts.

A Final Word about the Therapist

I have described what you should look for in picking a therapist to help your child. Clearly, you want a well-trained professional. But possibly more important, you and your child will want someone with whom you can relate. Therapy remains an extremely important and personal experience. Therapy may be the only time in your child's life that he or she becomes involved with any one individual in so close and intimate a manner. For this reason alone, it is crucial to ensure that the experience is a positive one. Often therapy appears not to be working, not because the therapy itself is at fault but because of a failure of the therapist and the client(s) to develop rapport. The following will help you remember the essential differences between the various therapists:

Social Worker = Therapy

Child psychologist = Therapy + psychological testing

Child psychiatrist = Therapy + diagnosis* +

medication/hospitalization

POINTS TO REMEMBER

In picking a therapist and involving your child in psychotherapy, have you done the following:

☐ Checked the credentials of the therapist?
☐ Found out what experience the therapist has had working with children with similar problems?

☐ Discussed the possible use of psychological testing from the viewpoint of objectives and information gained?

---

*Distinguishing between the psychological-behavioral problem caused primarily by an emotional factor and one caused by an organic factor.

☐ Developed a therapeutic contract that you and your child (when age-appropriate) can agree on, involving among other things cost, time, goals, and commitment?

☐ Discussed the possible use of medication?

☐ Discussed the use of a school contact and visit, home visit, or any environmental visit should it be useful toward better understanding and helping your child?

☐ Discussed your involvement, as part of the therapeutic contract, in the therapy?

If you have not done any one of the above, do so before you and your child make a commitment to psychological treatment for the child.

The Mental Health Agency

Your child may have to use the psychological services offered by a mental health agency. This may be a public mental health agency sponsored by a governmental unit (e.g., the state) or a private, nonprofit group. The proliferation during the past ten years of mental health agencies to provide a variety of psychological services to children and their families has been astonishing. Prior to that time, most nonprivate mental health services were provided either through the community mental health clinic system or through a limited number of child guidance clinics along with a few independent nonprofit groups.

The community mental health clinic system was established in the 1960s in an attempt to provide mental health services in a more universal way, with the country subdivided into catchment areas (geographical areas containing a certain number of people). The hope was that more people would have psychological help available. It had been characteristic then as now, that these services (usually offered privately) were concentrated in certain areas (most often urban). It represented an attempt to spread out the availability of these services. The child guidance clinic model that had been developed long before the mental health clinic system was not directly supported by a governmental unit and thus was not directly accountable to the population it served. The focus of the child guidance clinic, as the name implied, was to guide parents and children through the growing-up process.

Subsequently, many other agencies and groups have developed in order to offer services to children and their families. The confusion over which agency to use seems appropriate. There is no formal rating system to help families determine which of these agencies provide quality care. Although many agencies are mandated to provide services in various psychological areas, the quality of those services is variable. Often, community mental health clinics are stronger in the area of adult services than children's services because of an inability to find qualified professionals. In any comparison between a private professional and a public agency, the following points must be taken into consideration.

1. *The child's psychological needs.* Picking any specific agency must be based on the child's psychological needs. The recommendation to use an agency as opposed to a professional in private practice may be made because of a specific individual who works in that agency. Here again the decision is based on the reputation of the individual therapist. At times, your child may be referred to an agency with no specific therapist named. This is the least desirable way to obtain services (just as in the situation when we discussed being referred to a hospital without a specific physician being identified). Knowing a particular therapist's name allows you to help the child receive better services. Also, there is a line of accountability between the therapist suggested and the person who referred your child. We will discuss later how you can make sure that your child is seen by the recommended therapist.

2. *Money.* Psychological services for children, as previously mentioned, can be costly. Therapy and counseling may take a long time, sometimes years, to reach desired goals and permanent improvement. Although individual therapy sessions may not seem costly, the continuing cost over time can mount up rapidly. If therapy becomes a financial burden, alternatives to private therapy may have to be found. Thus, one reason for turning to an agency is cost. Most agencies provide services on a sliding-scale fee system. The fee charged is based on the total income of the family, taking into account the number of members in the

family. Even at the highest rate, the charge is usually far less than that of a private therapist. Some agencies, such as those supported by governmental units (relying on taxes), will provide services without cost if you cannot afford to pay. Services provided by an agency are often covered by health insurance. In discussing the cost of receiving psychological services from an agency, you may wish to compare private and public help.

3. *Special services.* In the area of special services, public agencies may have the edge over private therapists. These services include after-school play groups, Big Brother programs, and special summer programs. One reason why agencies have more information and direct knowledge of these special programs is that they are involved in developing and running them or, given the large population they serve, are knowledgeable of their existence. Often, the mental health agency can approach your child's problem from the "team" viewpoint. By having the social worker, psychologist, and possibly child psychiatrist all under the same roof, it is easier for them to work together as a team as opposed to attempting the same approach in the private sector. The cost of bringing these professionals together privately may be prohibitive. From a therapeutic standpoint, the agency can provide more options than an individual therapist. This can be seen in the availability of individual therapy, family therapy, group therapy (e.g., adolescent group or mother's support groups), or more "outward-bound" programs (therapist visits the house). Agencies can have good contact with schools in the area. This usually comes about from the frequency with which school or educational systems turn to local agencies for help. This can also be true in the area of the judicial system and family court. Many times, for instance, the family court has a collaborative relationship with a mental health agency. These agencies can thus become very helpful if your child is involved with family court and is felt to require mental health services.

The Initial Contact

As in seeking other services for your child, the initial contact is very important. Once again you will try to gain as much information as you can about services your child needs. When calling the mental health agency, state: "I was referred by (name of referring person), who said I should speak directly with (name of person you were referred to)." Many times, agencies have an intake process that includes talking initially to a different person who gathers information. Should the agency you called use a secretary for that purpose, after giving the identifying information, state: "I was told to speak with (name of therapist) about this problem." Other than gathering identifying information (e.g., name and age of the child), there is no appropriate reasons to say any more about the child's situation to anyone other than the therapist to whom you were referred.

Obviously, when choosing to deal with an agency, you have to put up with a certain amount of bureaucracy that is not associated with using a private therapist. However, do not let the red tape discourage you. Instead, be persistent in your demand to speak with the therapist. Inform the secretary, if necessary, of the immediacy of the problem. If you cannot speak with the therapist immediately, ask: "How long before (name of therapist) will be able to contact me?" The secretary should be able to give you a good idea how long it will take the person to call back.

REMEMBER: If it takes over twenty-four hours for the therapist to call you back, that tells you about the therapist's commitment to you given that there was no unusual emergency.

If the secretary informs you that you will be sent an application that has to be returned before you can make an appointment, find another agency, regardless of the recommendation. When you speak to the recommended therapist, say who recommended you to him or her. Clearly state the nature of the problem and let the therapist know the kind of services you need. State: "We have a family problem," or "My son doesn't get along well in school." By briefly defining the presenting problem, the therapist can let you know whether he or his agency is appropriate to help your child. If it is not, ask: "Could you suggest another agency that can work with my child and her kind of problem?"

At the time of the initial call or when you speak to the therapist, an appointment will be set up for you and the child. If the appointment is more than two weeks away, ask: "Do you think my child can wait that long?" This should let the therapist know that you feel the problem is serious. If the therapist is unable to move up the appointment, you will have to appraise the situation and decide whether you want to continue with this therapist. If not, ask: "Who else or what agency might be able to see my child sooner?"

Should the child's problem be of an emergency nature, you may need to be seen on an emergency basis. In general, a "good" agency should have the capacity to handle emergency situations. However, as in other emergency services, you may not be seen by the person suggested or recommended. Emergency services are often based on the idea of trying to squeeze you in. After all, if you had an appointment with a therapist, you wouldn't want to be displaced by another client. A good agency should have an emergency walk-in system that allows the youngster and family to be seen during the day of the crisis.

Once you have set up an appointment, you need to prepare yourself just as you did in the case of seeking out a private therapist. Coming to the initial appointment with a clear, written outline of the problem ensures you that you will tell the whole story and not leave out an important fact or date. Upon meeting the therapist, it is important to have some information about this person. You should ask: "Although you were recommended highly, I would feel more comfortable if you would tell me something about yourself." A good therapist should not react defensively to this statement. Rather, the therapist should realize that telling you something about himself or herself will make you more comfortable and thus a more cooperative ally in the therapeutic process.

Things You Will Want to Know About the Agency

Although a therapist may not have any one therapeutic approach to children in treatment, the agency in which he or she works may have one. Many agencies approach a psychological problem from a collaborative point of view, with one therapist working with the child and another working with the parent. There are theoretical justifications for doing this, and often this approach can lead to excellent therapeutic results. However, it is important for you to find out what approaches the agency will take in working with your child. Since agencies offer many more types of therapies than a private therapist, you should ask: "What types of treatment might my child receive here?" If the therapist talks about only one approach, beware. This often means that the agency will try to squeeze you and the child into its therapeutic model rather than attempting to adapt its approach to the child's needs. Inflexible systems are the least likely to succeed.

It is important that you understand how the therapist will go about determining the psychological needs of your child and thus the appropriate treatment. Unlike the private therapist, agencies often will approach your child with a team of professionals. It is not unusual for the child to ultimately be seen by an adult psychiatrist, a child psychiatrist (when one is available), or a child psychologist. Furthermore, many agencies make it standard policy to have the information obtained in the initial interview presented to a group of professionals who constitute the staff of the agency.

Many families are fearful that such a presentation will jeopardize their confidentiality. It is important to ask: "Will my child and his problems be discussed with any other staff?" At this point, you will be told what the policy of this agency is in dealing with a new case. Although confidentiality is usually not a problem, the use of an agency in a small community, where some staff members may be known socially to you outside the agency, can force you to request that this routine procedure be bypassed. Whether the agency can abide by this change in rules should be discussed. Another important point raised in asking the preceeding question is whether the recommended therapist or the person you are seeing is supervised by a more experienced therapist. If so, find out who that person is and his or her training background. Furthermore, you may want to meet that person. You have a right to request such a meeting.

REMEMBER: That person is making decisions about your child and you.

By sharing your child's information with others, the therapist can gain from the various inputs of the other professional staff. No therapist can be aware of all facets of the therapeutic process. The team approach can speed up the process of therapy by pointing out early unseen potential problems. Furthermore, if a problem arises between you, your child, and the therapist, you may wish to talk with someone else in the hopes of straightening out the conflict. By having another staff person(s) involved on an ongoing basis, you can talk to that person without having to recount the entire history and progress of therapy. You can request such a meeting by saying: "I'm finding it difficult to communicate with you. Who else can help us in this matter?" An experienced therapist should be able to look at the situation and determine whether your request is valid. If you feel so, persist in your conviction. The third-party mediator may, however, find the problem to be *you*, not the therapist.

Labeling

Agencies are required to give diagnostic labels to children's problems so that they can maintain their records. Because of the funding mechanism, it is vital for them to keep accurate records of the number and types of children they see on an ongoing basis. A diagnostic label can be useful if it helps define the area in which a child is struggling emotionally. Diagnostic labels are part of the psychological vocabulary of mental health professionals. By using a diagnostic label, professionals are able to quickly determine the general area in which a child is having a problem.

Unfortunately, labels are misused many times. Various types of professionals (psychologists and psychiatrists) can define the same label in a variety of ways. Thus, what it may mean to one professional or group of professionals may be different from what it means to another. It is not supposed to work that way, but it does, mainly because labels can depend a lot more on subjective criteria than objective criteria. Furthermore, labels conjure up misconceptions based on the training, experience, and biases of the professional(s) receiving this information about a child. Thus, labeling your child, giving the child a "quick reference title," can be detrimental. It can categorize the child before giving him or her a chance to be evaluated as an individual by each new professional.

Labels also can last a lifetime, becoming part of the child's permanent record. This information, given the computerized world we live in, can become part of an insurance form, a school record, or a general health questionnaire early in a child's life and remain there into adulthood. Often, the label can become a part of the record, about which the child may have so little information that he or she cannot explain the circumstances of its origin. In general, labels are restrictive. Thus, it is very important that you find out how the therapist is going to label your child for the purpose of recordkeeping. Many times, the real need for labeling may be to satisfy health insurance forms so that you or the agency can receive reimbursement. If that is the situation, the least restrictive label should be adequate.

If the agency needs a label for its records, you should ask the therapist: "What label will you have to use to describe my child's problem?" This should let the therapist know that you are aware that as part of any agency's policy (it is important that you ask this question of a private therapist as well), the therapist is required to label your child. If the therapist asks you why that is important for you to know, reply: "How you label my child is a serious decision. It is a label that will be in her records forever and possibly follow her without her control." The therapist should be able to explain the meaning of the label. You should ask: "Is calling him this name (label) going to be a problem for him elsewhere or later on in life?" By repeating this statement, you again notify the therapist that you have real concerns about labeling your child other than in the least restrictive way. The therapist may say: "These records on your child are confidential. Only trained professionals can see them."

REMEMBER: If the therapist has not brought up the point of record confidentiality, you should.

Basically, records are confidential. In agencies, however, many people who are not directly involved in your child's case can have access to them. Agencies should have a policy about releasing information. This will require you to sign release forms identifying which individuals or agencies (e.g., the school) you wish this information to be shared with. In discussing the sharing of information, ask: "Is it important that all this information be shared with these people or would it be better if only some parts of it were shared?"

Often, we tend to *overshare* information with others. Once reports are written and tests given, it is just *easier* to photostat the whole record than to write a new record that contains just the essential or appropriate data. In sending the whole record, you cannot be sure that it will be read only by the appropriate individuals. Furthermore, unless the therapist knows the training background of the person being sent the information, he or she cannot be sure that the individual reading the basic data will arrive at the same conclusions as the therapist. Although there is no guarantee that you can control the types of records sent in a release of information, you can make your desires known to the therapist. You can ask for a copy of the record so that you will have some idea of what information is being shared. You may simply have to trust the therapist, however, given the fact that you have chosen him or her to care for your child.

Agencies have an additional difficulty dealing with confidentiality. Unlike private therapists, they have only one set of records about the child. A private therapist can say one thing in formal records and maintain other information to be stored in his or her head or even in private records. This is often a protection against subpoenas by courts should your child's records or psychological information need to be part of the judicial process (custody proceedings or juvenile crime). Agencies have to maintain these records.

REMEMBER: The therapist does not work as an individual. The therapist works for the *agency.*

The records do not belong to the therapist but to the agency. Continuity of these records is the responsibility ultimately of the agency. Should the therapist leave, the records remain with the agency, where they are available if either you or your child needs them. When records become second-generation, (i.e., should the first therapist leave and you and your child continue with a second therapist), the records become the responsibility of the new therapist. At this point, information gained by the new therapist is put in the records. At times, it may conflict with information, impressions, and perceptions made by the first therapist. Thus, records, while meant to compile information, can also be an account of changing therapists.

Things to Keep in Mind About Labels, Records, and Confidentiality

☐ Have you asked the therapist what label he or she will give your child? Is this the least restrictive label that can be used?

☐ Have you asked who will have access to the records in the agency? (This is especially important in a small community.)

☐ Have you asked how long records are kept and what protection your child has that after the therapist leaves, the information will be protected?

☐ Have you asked whether certain parts of the record can be marked "confidential," or not to be shared?

☐ Have you asked whether
the whole record is sent to
an individual or agency
requesting information

about your child? Or will the
record be summarized?
(This is a better way to
handle it!)

One final point about records. At times, you will want to read
the record. If you have a question about the record or want to know
what is in it, the therapist should be willing to discuss it with you.
Reading a record with psychological jargon in it can be misleading.
The record is a formal document about your child's psychological
development. It is very important and should be respected. It should
not be taken lightly, and information placed in it should be determined carefully. Parents who have received full copies of reports
have become confused and angry. In these situations, summaries
would be more useful.

POINTS TO REMEMBER

- *Why you go to a mental health agency.* The most frequent reasons
for using a mental health agency are: (1) financial (agencies cost
less), (2) reputation of the agency or of an individual therapist working in the agency, and (3) special services that are not available
through a private therapist.
- *The therapist.* If you use a mental health agency, can you be seen
by the person you want, or is that not up to you? Ask: "Do the
agency's policies dictate the type of therapy my child will receive,
or is that decision based on the child's needs?" For instance, can a
family agency that provides family therapy (working with the family
unit) also see a child in individual therapy if it is appropriate?
- *Schedule and fees.* Find out during the initial visit the cost to you
and how this cost is based on your income. In discussing the frequency of visits to the therapist, ask whether the frequency is based
on agency policy. Some agencies have a schedule that allows your
child to be seen, for instance, only every two weeks.
- *Continuity.* It is important to remember that unlike a private
therapist, an agency may change therapists even after therapy has
begun. Many times, therapists go on to other jobs, or policy change
in an agency can shift them to other areas. It does not mean that

you and your child cannot become involved again in a positive way with a new therapist. However, it can be a disruptive process.

Hot Lines

In the past ten years, the number of hot lines that have been established is astounding. The number of prerecorded telephone messages you can dial to receive help has also proliferated. Few communities are without access to a hot line number. If a local community has not developed such a number, usually there is a number that can be easily reached at the state level. Hot lines were essentially set up to help parents obtain information. Many times, hot lines were established to provide a service directly to you or your child during a crisis. The variety of services or information afforded a telephone caller is astonishing. The problem with a hot line is that often people are not aware that they exist, and thus you do not take advantage of the service offered. In talking about hot lines, it is important to realize that they can be utilized in a number of ways.

Crisis
You probably are well aware that hot lines are useful in terms of crisis. As the name implies, they allow the sharing of information, advice, or even counseling during a time of crisis. This allows you to get help quickly. Although the community may have only a limited number of hot lines, others have many different kinds. They are available for you or your child, especially the adolescent. The following is a list of the most popular types of crisis hot lines:

• *Poison control.* Most communities have a poison control center. This center should be able to quickly provide you with information about a substance your child has ingested, inhaled, or touched that might be poisonous or otherwise dangerous. Most often, these poison control centers are located in hospitals so that the most professional advice can be obtained.
• *Drugs.* Many communities provide a hot line number to be called if your child has taken a drug that is having an adverse effect (a nonprescription drug or "street substance"). You and the child

(usually an adolescent) should be aware of this number in case of an emergency. The child should be encouraged to call this number even without your knowledge should he or she be involved with a drug that is having a negative effect on the body or mind.

● *Child abuse.* Child abuse hot lines have become increasingly popular, and the number of reported incidents of child abuse has increased greatly. Many such hot lines encourage their use before the actual act of child abuse has occurred. Many times parenting becomes very frustrating and can lead to overuse of physical punishment. Child abuse hot lines hope that before you reach that point, you will call.

● *Runaways.* Hot lines for runaways have been set up locally and also tie into national hot lines. The number of youngsters running away from home each year is alarming (well over 1 million) and does not even take into account the number of youngsters who run away and are never reported. By discussing this hot line with your child ahead of time, especially if you believe that the child might run away, you develop a means of communication. The hot line attempts, through continual communication, to reduce family tensions during a runaway. By allowing you and the child to talk to each other in a nonthreatening and indirect manner, the hope is that more constructive plans for resolving the differences between you and the child can be arranged.

● *Rape and sexual abuse.* Should your child be subjected to rape or sexual abuse, it is important that you obtain clear and appropriate information about how to help. Besides receiving medical advice (which often means going to the local hospital, especially in the case of rape), psychological counseling is most important. Since the people providing the information are used to the types of situations you will be calling about, they can give you direct advice on how to help. Once again, if the child is an adolescent, this number should be made available to use whether or not you are aware that the child has called it.

● *Suicide.* Suicide hot lines were probably one of the first types of hot lines to be set up. They are meant to defuse an obviously life-threatening situation. Most suicide hot lines are manned by people who have had special training in dealing with suicidal individuals over the phone. Again, your child should be aware that such a hot line exists, to be called if the need should arise.

• *Pregnancy and birth control.* Your child may want information about pregnancy and birth control. The hot line can often provide that information, preventing the child from involving herself or himself in a situation that may be harmful to his or her health. Once again, it is important that your teenage daughter or son be aware of the hot line and that he or she can use it, without your knowledge if necessary.

General Information

Although initially thought of as providing information or services in times of crises, hot lines are now being used more and more for noncrisis services. Much of the information is about services available in your community or state. One such type of hot line is called an Info Line, which currently is being set up nationwide to provide communities with readily accessible information. These types of hot lines can provide information in the areas of the physical, educational, legal, and psychological needs of children. Some of the information you and your child can obtain are in the following areas:

Drugs
Alcohol abuse
Psychological counseling
Handicapped children's services
Advocacy
Day-care centers
Schools
Housing
Human sexuality information
Legal services
Venereal disease
Mental health services

The hot line offers you the opportunity to find out information concerning a particular area when you have no other options. Often, hot line information can be more up to date than information you might receive from a "professional," since hot lines have to be kept as well-informed as possible. Given the greater volume of people they serve, it is very important that they keep up to date. Should you be moving from one city to another and have a question about a particular service, you may want to call that community's hot line before moving. At least it can give you some information with which to start.

How to Use the Hot Line
When using the hot line, it is important that you remember the following:

● *Information.* Before calling, identify your child's needs as clearly as possible. If this requires knowing dates, names, and any other identifying information, write that information down. The more clearly you can define the needs, the faster and better able the hot line will be able to provide you with the information. In many ways, a hot line can be much like the yellow pages in the telephone book. In this case, the hot line does the walking. Obviously, if you use the hot line at times of crisis, you may not yet have all the facts. The hot line will be able to advise you how to go about collecting information to share with them. Many times, it may take you more than one call to the hot line to give necessary information and obtain the desired answers.

● *How good the information is.* After identifying yourself to the person who answers your hot line call, you should expect an answer to your questions. If you don't get one, the hot line should be able to tell you how to do this. Do not hesitate to ask the person on the hot line to identify himself. You can do this by stating: "It would help me to know who I am speaking with. Are you a volunteer or full-time staff member?" You should not expect a name unless the person has been instructed by the people who run the hot line to give it. Many times, full-time staff members will readily identify themselves. They should always be able to tell you their professional background, *if any*. Many hot lines, out of necessity, use nonprofessional volunteers. The reason for asking the above question is to determine how much credence you can put on the information you will obtain. Should you be calling for legal advice and talk with a lawyer, obviously you can give more weight to the information. On the other hand, if you are seeking medical advice from a nonmedical person, you will have to decide how much credence you can place on the information.

REMEMBER: Hot lines are not meant to give you specific advice. Rather, they were set up to help you find that information from the most reliable source. When you call a hot line and speak with an individual who gives out specific advice on a matter, carefully question that information. It may be wrong.

Once you have identified your child's needs, ask: "Is this the type of problem or service you get many calls on?" The hot line person may say: "Yes! We get a lot of calls for this," or "No, only once in a while." Obviously, the more frequently the hot line is asked to provide information about a specific problem or service, the more likely it is that they have information that is up to date and can be considered reasonably reliable.

• *Identifying yourself.* You are not required to give any specific identifying information about yourself to the hot line, such as your name, your child's name, or your address. Hot lines may require some general information about you and your child (age, religion, etc.) so that they can maintain their records. When calling a hot line, it is important to ask: "Who else will be involved with the information I give you?" In some situations, such as child abuse, the hot line may have a legal obligation to report calls to the appropriate authorities. Usually, the authorities notified are trained to handle such situations and can be very helpful.

• *Diagnosing or labeling.* Under no circumstance should you accept a diagnosis or the labeling of a situation over a hot line. At times, this can happen should you come in contact with an overzealous worker. At best, the hot line person can say: "It sounds as if. . . ." This should help you find more specific information.

• *Recommendations.* It is important to ask: "Do you make recommendations or have preferences when giving out information?" Many hot line personnel are not allowed to give personal preference of service. For instance, should you be calling to get information about day care centers in your community, the hot line may have a list of centers with no stated preferences. Others may have a rating list. Ask: "Does your information also tell about the quality of the services?" or "Have you received any specific complaints about any of these services you have listed?" The hot line person can answer that question more directly. Other times, the person will state that there is a policy against giving any specific preference.

• *Hot line to hot line.* Hot lines tend to have an informal network between themselves. This allows one hot line to call another to obtain information. If your child runs away to another community and you are aware of where he or she went, the hot line in your community can call the hot line in the other community and attempt to find out information that may be helpful in bringing the child back.

• *Bad drugs.* If you child is having adverse reaction to drugs received in another community, the hot line in your community can contact the drug hot line in that area. They can obtain information about possible "bad drugs" you child may have taken, since other young people in that community may have turned to the drug hot line for help.

Your Child and the Hot Line

The hot line can be used by your child (especially an adolescent) during a crisis. Hot lines can be perceived as neutral parties in an adolescent crisis or conflict. You can suggest to your child that he or she call the hot line (or visit it since many have walk-in services) to ventilate or gain information. In this way, you can help direct the child to a responsible group rather than allow the child to resolve an adolescent crisis alone or with peers. If there is time and adequate warning about an impending crisis, you may wish to call the hot line yourself beforehand. This allows you to talk to the hot line people and learn how they go about advising your child should he or she call.

Often, if you call and know that there is a strong likelihood that you child will call the hot line, you can leave some limited identifying information. Many hot lines have bulletin boards about individuals who might use or are repeatedly using the hot line. This allows them to direct certain callers to certain hot line personnel who are either better equipped professionally to handle a specific problem or have developed a special relationship with the caller. This information about your child can be useful in resolving the problem constructively. Furthermore, by calling ahead you can find out what the hot line can and cannot do when advising your child (e.g., if your child is under a certain age, do they have to contact you?)

The quality of advice given over the phone depends on the qualifications of the person to whom you speak; however, hot lines can give advice based on previous experiences with children like yours. At times, if you believe that your child has been using a hot line, you can call to find out whether he or she has contacted the hot line or has visited the hot line offices. Although the information that your child shares with the hot line should be considered confidential, it may be useful to know that your child is attempting to resolve a problem with others.

Certainly, encouraging your child to use hot line groups in the case of drugs is not only helpful but life-saving. Hot lines are well aware of the types of drugs that are on the street at any one time and usually can quickly advise your child about the possibility of life-threatening or harmful types circulating at that time. The use of the hot line for birth control and pregnancy information can also be beneficial. At times, adolescents need to talk with nonparental figures, especially in the area of sexuality. Hot lines usually provide information as to where to receive appropriate services such as sex counseling.

Check Out a Hot Line

The first way to check out the qualifications of a hot line is to find out who sponsors it. It may be a totally voluntary organization with no formal affiliation to any agency, private or public. Often, state and local governments recognize the community's need for a hot line and sponsor such a service. Obviously, an agency sponsored by a governmental unit or affiliated with a respected human services agency is more likely to provide higher-quality services and thus be more reliable.

POINTS TO REMEMBER

• Hot lines were set up to provide information during crisis and noncrisis situations. Their primary duty is to help you and your child link up with existing services and, in some cases, to help you hurdle the bureaucratic barriers that may be preventing the child from receiving help.
• Before using a hot line, check it out. If you don't have time, you have to listen carefully to the information you are receiving. When calling, if at all possible, talk to the same person each time for the

sake of continuity. It may mean you have to call back during that person's shift on the hot line.

● Hot lines are most useful for the following situations:

Crisis with no other information resources available.

To help defuse what appears as an unresolvable adolescent crisis in which communication between you and your child has failed.

To obtain information about services in a community that you do not presently live in, one you may be moving to, or one in which your child may be temporarily living (as a runaway or in boarding school).

If you are looking for information about a service for your child but don't know where to start to look for it.

● Make your child aware of the hot lines in your community. It may not only help your child but his or her friends as well should they need help and feel that they can not come to you or their parents.

REMEMBER: Hot lines can be used by all people. Unfortunately, many people view them as providing services for the disadvantaged. They are there for you and your child.

Index

achievement testing, 102
additives, in food, 39–46
admission requirements, for
    school, 96
advocacy hot lines, 158
agencies, *see* mental health
    agencies
alcohol abuse hot lines, 158
allies:
    in emergency rooms, 16–17
    in hospitals, 26
American Academy of Pediatrics, 8
analgesics, 35–36
answering services, 7
arrest, *see* legal needs
attendance requirements, for
    school, 96

baby teeth, 32
behavior management, 110
behavioral interventions, 134–135
birth control hot lines, 158

cafeterias, *see* lunchrooms
calendars, school, 97

carbohydrates, 40
cavities, tooth, 36
child abuse hot lines, 157
child life workers, 29
child psychiatrists, *see*
    psychiatrists
children:
    educational needs of, 61–108
    legal needs of, 47–60
    physical needs of, 1–46
    psychological needs of, 109–163
children's hospitals, 22
chronological immaturity, 99
classrooms:
    visiting, 68–69
    what to look for, 69–74
clinical child psychologists, 128
color recognition skills, 101
community hospitals, 4–5, 23
complications, medical, 19
confidentiality, 153–155
contracts, *see* therapeutic contracts
corporal punishment, 76
counseling, *see* therapists
courts, family, 57–58

165